ATLANTIC CITY
125 YEARS OF OCEAN MADNESS

8/21/05

To Philip,

    A simple Keepsake...

Take care + God Bless.

Always,

Mila

(MILA MATEO AGPAOA)

magpaoa2004 @ YAHOO.COM

(609) 348-0014

ATLANTIC CITY
125 YEARS OF OCEAN MADNESS

*Starring Miss America, Mr. Peanut,
Lucy the Elephant, the High Diving Horse,
and four generations of Americans cutting loose*

SECOND EDITION
PRODUCED AND COMPILED BY
VICKI GOLD LEVI

TEXT BY
LEE EISENBERG

ORIGINATED BY
ROD KENNEDY AND SUSAN SUBTLE DINTENFASS

TEN SPEED PRESS
BERKELEY, CALIFORNIA

TEN SPEED PRESS
P.O. Box 7123
Berkeley, California 94707

Original design by Kenneth Kneitel
Revised design and cover by Nancy Austin and Catherine Jacobes

MR. PEANUT
is a registered trademark of Nabisco, Inc.

MONOPOLY®
is a registered trademark of Parker Brothers
for its real estate trading game © 1994.
Parker Brothers is a division of Tonka Corporation,
Beverly, Massachusetts.

Library of Congress Cataloging-in-Publication Data
Levi, Vicki Gold.
Atlantic City: 125 Years of Ocean Madness /
by Vicki Gold Levi and Lee Eisenberg.
p.   cm.
Includes index.
ISBN 0-89815-613-0
1. Atlantic City (N.J.)—History.   2. Seaside resorts—New Jersey—
Atlantic City—History—19th century.   3. Seaside resorts—New Jersey—
Atlantic City—History—20th century.   I. Eisenberg, Lee, 1946– .   II. Title.
F144.A8L6   1994
974.9'85—dc20   93-46513
CIP

FIRST PRINTING 1994

Printed in the United States of America

2   3   4   5 — 98   97   96

THIS BOOK IS LOVINGLY DEDICATED TO AL GOLD,

CHIEF PHOTOGRAPHER OF ATLANTIC CITY

FROM 1939 TO 1964.

THE SECOND EDITION OF THIS BOOK

IS ALSO DEDICATED TO THE MEMORY

OF DR. ARTHUR DINTENFASS.

ACKNOWLEDGEMENTS

The pictures and words that appear in this book could never have been gathered and put down on paper without the generous assistance of a great number of people. To line all of them up and say thank you would require the length of ten Boardwalks and another 125 years. So if you helped us and somehow we lost you in the crowd, accept our sincerest apology and deepest appreciation.

For help on both the first and second editions of this book, we offer special thanks to the many photographers whose pictures appear throughout these pages, particularly to the late Fred and Myron Hess of Fred Hess and Son and Morris Newstat of Central Studies in Atlantic City. And we likewise acknowledge the men and women who wrote the newspaper accounts, articles, and books that tell the story of Atlantic City. In particular, we wish to cite Charles E. Funnell's *By the Beautiful Sea* (Alfred A. Knopf, 1975); Frank Deford's *There She Is* (Viking Press, 1971); William McMahon's *So Young...So Gay* (Atlantic City Press, 1970); Frank Butler's *Book of the Boardwalk* (1954 Association, Inc., Atlantic City, 1953).

We thank Anthony J. Kutschera, whose love of Atlantic City's past provided much insight into the resort's architecture and social history; Michele Gold Johnson, who worked tirelessly to collect material on the West Coast; Sue Maggs, who opened her doors and gave us a temporary Atlantic City home.

We thank Frank Havens and Jimmy Hamid for pointing us in the right direction and for supplying us with a trove of pictures; Jimmie McCullough and Lou Cunningham for their unfailing memories and endless patience; Mr. and Mrs. Joseph Hackney and their daughter, Marion, for their boundless information and love; Adrian Phillips, whose command of Atlantic City history kept us on firm footing; Art Gager, Jr., of Fralinger's for setting us straight on saltwater taffy; Cynthia Ringe, whose excellent oral histories for the Atlantic City Free Library enable much to survive; Pat Ehrhardt and Ronnie Douglas of the Feinstein/Kutschera Realty Company for taking our messages; the staff at Hess Photography for providing excellent prints of frail images; Pat Dahme, Veronica and Lois Anderson for all kinds of research and assistance; Arnette and Jake French for their memories of life in the Steel Pier Water Circus; Harry J. Katz for clearing the way with the Philadelphia newspapers; Beverly Gold for sharing her past with her researcher daughter; Eve Greenfield for taking her son to the shore, where he loved the smell of the air.

We thank Maureen Sherr Frank, Marie Boyd, Dian Spitler, Christine King, Lawrie Nomer, and the able staff at the Atlantic City Free Library and Heston Research Room; Betty and Fred Ehrhardt and the volunteer staff at the Atlantic County Historical Society; Paul Learn, Ed Hitzel, Sonny Schwartz, and Hennie Logan at the *Press of Southern New Jersey*; Dr. Alia Sayegh and her 1978 humanities class at Atlantic City High School; Mary Morgan at the Greater Chamber of Commerce of Atlantic City; everyone at the Atlantic City Press Bureau, and the city's Department of Public Relations; Bill Cowart, Red Ritson, and Matt Custer at Atlantic Electric; Albert Marks, Jr., Ruth McCandliss, Katie Ryan, Leonard Horn, Karen Aarons, Bill Caligari, Mary McGinnis, and Carol Plum at the Miss America

Pageant; and the board of directors at the Atlantic City Historical Museum on Garden Pier. Josephine Herron of the Save Lucy Committee, Inc.; Peter Parker at the Historical Society of Pennsylvania; Charles Cummings at the Newark Public Library; Reed Abel at the Edison National Historic Site; the staffs of the Theatre Collection of the New York Public Library, the Library of Congress, the New Jersey Historical Society in Newark; Alicia Stamm at the Historical American Buildings Survey in Washington; Doris Vinton of the Ziegfeld Club; Debbie Foster of the H.J. Heinz Company; Michele Jordan and Susan Fedyck of the Rowland Company, New York; Carol Steinkarus at Parker Brothers; Helen Clifton at David Jacobson Associates, Atlantic City; John Bowstead at Alan Lapidus Associates, New York; and Ken Weatherford and Michael L. B. Lacy at *Atlantic City Magazine*.

We thank the casino industry for their help: Bally's Park Place Casino and Tower, Caesars Atlantic City Hotel and Casino, Claridge Casino Hotel, The Grand, A Bally's Casino Resort, Harrah's Casino Hotel, Merv Griffin's Resorts Casino Hotel, Sands Hotel and Casino, Showboat Casino and Hotel, TropWorld Casino and Entertainment Resort, Trump's Castle Casino Resort, Trump Plaza Hotel and Casino, and Trump Taj Mahal Casino Resort.

We thank for their help, encouragement, and friendship: Phyllis Ahlstead, Linda Arking Avila, Anita Barrion, Magdy Barsoum, Mrs. Herbert E. Brooks, Jeff Brown, Anna Burak, Richard Burt, Harold Care, Ellen and Michael Cohen, Neil Cohen,Commissioner Edmund Colanzi, Marilyn and Alvin Cooperman, Grace and Willy D'Amato, Paul "Skinny" D'Amato, Dolores and Herb Danska, Margaret and Charles Doble, Jr., Mrs. James Durante, Tony Edgeworth, Linda Eisenberg, Ray Farkas, Audrey and Norman Fischer, Doris Flagg, Redenia Gilliam-Mosee, Edith and Ralph Green, Ed Grusheski, Jeanette Hall, Sue and Mark Haven, Jean Herrmann, Joyce Jurnovoy, Trudy Kaplan, Bea Kershenblatt, Mary Korey, Debbie Kornblau, Pinky Kravitz, Kathy Kutschera, Steve Lawrence, Jan Heller Levi, Lillian Levy, Gloria Loomis, Farida Mahmood, Joe Mansi, Jeffrey Marinoff, Bill McCullough, Marie McCullough, Margaret McGee, Wayne Clay Meeks, Susan and Don Meredith, Florence Valore Miller, Marvin Miller, Nena O'Neil, Reese Palley, Chloe Price, Cindy Mason Purdie, Adelina Richardson, Joyce and Robert Ruffolo, Lucille Russo, Henrietta Sheldon, April Silver, Joan Savitt Sless, Steven Sless, Louis Solomon, Mitzi and Harry Stein, Gail Stern, Herbert Stern, Russell Taylor, Russell Thaw, Kim Tieger, Anne Coleman Torrey, Minnie Hess Trilling, Sidney Trusty, LaVerne Usry, Tressa Verna, Wendel White, and Sandy Williamson.

We thank the people of Clarkson N. Potter, publishers of the first edition of this book, for their unflagging commitment: Jane West, Michael Fragnito, Pam Pollack, and Ellen Gilbert. We are especially grateful to Carolyn Hart Bryant, who was the first to see the possibilities, and to Carol Southern, whose gracious editing becalmed the madness.

We thank Ken Kneitel for his original design of the first edition of this book and Ron Lieberman for illustrating the original cover.

We thank agent Peter Miller for his determined efforts throughout both editions; and Robert Asman for photographic reproductions the second time around.

We thank Phil Wood, publisher of Ten Speed Press, and his capable staff for giving this book new life: George Young, Christine Carswell, Nancy Austin, Catherine Jacobes, and Hal Hershey.

And finally we thank Alex and Adam Levi, who pretended to believe the promise that one day the clutter would disappear and there would be, in its place, a book.

CONTENTS

Atlantic City before the Boardwalk, circa 1860.

By the Desolate Sea

It was the last stop on a railroad to nowhere, a city built on sand. There is no legend to explain why it is where it is, no mythology to gussy up its origin. It was built there because *there* happened to be the shortest distance between Philadelphia and the sea, between urban congestion and salt breezes, between hundreds of thousands of people and a handful of men who knew a good thing when they saw one. And before the sixty miles of track were laid between the City of Brotherly Love and the Queen of Resorts, it was nowhere, just sand and some marshes, a wilderness.

Absecon Island, where Atlantic City took place, was known to the Lenni Lenape Indians as *Absegami*, or "Little Sea Water." The earliest white landowner was one Thomas Budd who, while a good Quaker farmer, was hardly a prophet. Colony leaders *forced* Budd to buy lots on *Absegami* as part of a deal to acquire fertile real estate on the mainland. The cost of this not-very-prime beachfront property: four cents an acre. The year was 1695, and Budd was as miserable as a MONOPOLY player who had just landed on Baltic. "Those swamps and dunes—not at any price! Be reasonable, gentlemen, what will those islands be good for—seagull nests?"

Thomas Budd thus became the first, but not the last, decent person to be conned out of small change on Absecon Island. Writing in 1904, on the occasion of Atlantic City's fiftieth anniversary, Dr. Thomas K. Reed described Budd's unhappy acquisition:

> It lay out beyond the silent marshes that are interspersed by bays.... In calm weather the stillness of the island was only broken by the subdued murmur of the sea, the honking of migrating water fowl and the screams of gulls as they hovered above the bars...of the day time tide....
>
> When it stormed and the wind was in the East, the waves pounded the strand in its rage, roaring like a hungry beast in a trackless desert.
>
> The whole island then trembled as in fear; moreover, when night came on, mysterious voices mingled with the ocean's mutterings.

In short, *Absegami* wasn't exactly a picture postcard. Nevertheless, there were those who saw possibilities. Jeremiah Leeds, the first volunteer to actually live on the island, arrived in 1838 to build a cedar log cabin on what would become, in fact, Baltic Avenue. Solid and snug, the dwelling was shingled on the outside and had grooved planks within. Keeping out the weather, not people, was the problem—and that suited Leeds just fine. From all accounts, he wasn't the most neighborly of souls, which explains why Leeds sank roots into the desert in the first place, why he didn't pack up and go home after Labor Day.

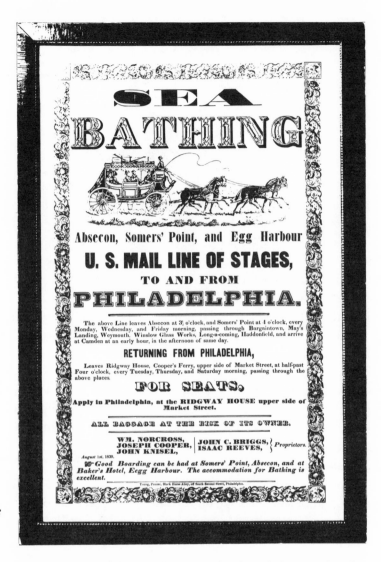

Until the coming of the railroad, Philadelphia and the Jersey shore were linked by stagecoach and ferry, as shown by an 1839 advertisement.

In 1850 there were only seven houses on Absecon Island, and the people who lived therein were considerably outnumbered by the blacksnakes that slithered among the brambles, by the mosquitoes that swarmed from May to September. Suddenly, something happened. Dr. Jonathan Pitney, a resident of a nearby mainland village, was approached by Richard Osborne, a civil engineer from Philadelphia. Osborne, a hard-headed schemer and master builder, had recently returned from a visit to the West, where he'd come down with a severe case of Manifest Destiny. Pitney, a gentleman with connections, was the physician who could treat the affliction—not with ointments and elixirs, but with propaganda and salesmanship.

A. L. English's history of Atlantic City (1884) is unsparing in its praise of Dr. Jonathan Pitney:

> There seems little doubt that [he] was the real founder of Atlantic City—the spirit that first appreciated its wonderful curative powers, and placed effectively before the capitalists its attractions as a watering place—dryness of atmosphere, bathing facilities, gunning, fishing and sailing privileges, with its proximity to

Philadelphia…. A desire sprang in [Pitney's] breast to make the delectable spot accessible to the great business centres of the Union….His faith was strong and his enthusiasm correspondingly great.

The grand United States Hotel, built in 1854. Ulysses S. Grant slept here, along with others who paid $3.50 a night for the privilege.

It was hello to the railroad, goodbye to the trackless desert, good riddance to *Absegami*. In the club rooms and offices of Philadelphia's most powerful, Pitney sang the virtues of the now "delectable" spot. He sang of air that could cure a thousand diseases, of summer cottages that would honor the sunrise, of untold millions of city refugees who'd one day beat the heat in the restorative surf. And as the melody lingered, it became clear: all this and more was possible, and at a reasonable price—sixty miles of iron track, some locomotives, cars, and cabooses, plus a couple of clerks selling tickets at either end.

As Pitney sang, Osborne mapped the route of the proposed railway. It would run from Camden to the as yet unnamed spa, which Osborne referred to as "Philadelphia's lungs." Enchanted investors stepped right up. In June of 1852, ten thousand Camden and Atlantic Railroad shares were sold, mainly to businessmen with factories or land holdings in the Absecon vicinity. Moreover, investors could also

At Schaufler's Hotel and Summer Gardens, 1879, railroad conductors from the nearby depot cried "All Aboard!" at the entrance to the saloon. Outside the hotel a bell sounded in the beer garden whenever a new keg was tapped. Inside, the guest rooms weren't posh, but they offered a good night's sleep after a generous nighcap.

acquire equity in the Camden and Atlantic Land Company, which was busily gathering up vast chunks of beachfront for so much play money.

In December 1853 Richard Osborne appeared before the railroad's board with his final plan. One of the items on the agenda was discussion of an official name, early favorites being Bath, Ocean City, Seabeach, and Surfing. Osborne, with characteristic flair, settled the matter. As he'd recall years after: "I unrolled a great and well-finished map of the…bathing place, [and] they saw in large letters of gold, stretching over the waves, the words, ATLANTIC CITY. This title was greeted with enthusiasm by the board. The name was unanimously adopted and that day 'Atlantic City' came into existence on paper."

Though some contend otherwise, most sources credit Richard Osborne with naming the streets along Atlantic City's beachfront. Running north and south, parallel to the ocean, are avenues named after the world's seas: Pacific, Atlantic, Arctic, Baltic, and Mediterranean. Avenues running east and west are named after America's states.

The governor of New Jersey approved Atlantic City's municipal charter on March 3, 1854. Four months later, on July 1, the first caravan steamed out of Camden, accompanied by brass bands and hoopla. The trip took a respectable two and a half hours, including time spent on a boat-crossing of Absecon Bay, which awaited a bridge.

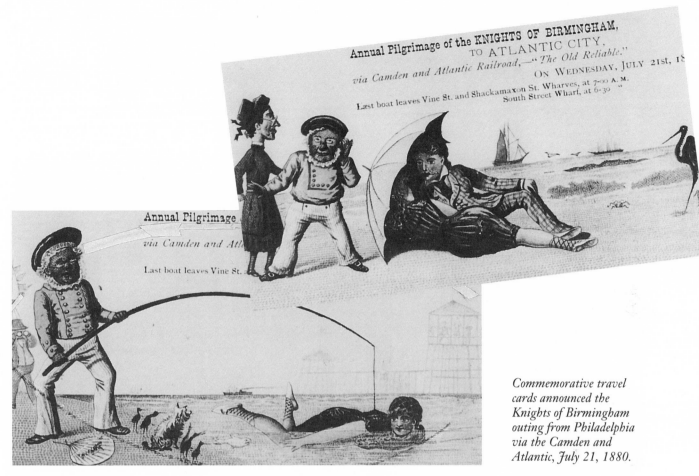

Commemorative travel cards announced the Knights of Birmingham outing from Philadelphia via the Camden and Atlantic, July 21, 1880.

Once on the other side, the six hundred reporters and dignitaries had little to do but kill time before the next train out. The season of '54 must be recorded as the shortest in Atlantic City's history. The resort's first hotels, or excursion houses, were largely unfinished, and the island was much the same as in Jeremiah Leeds's time. Joseph A. Barstow, who would come to settle and prosper in Atlantic City, had these traveler's impressions in early 1854:

> I had heard of Atlantic City, and one day thought I would make the trip down from Philadelphia out of curiosity. At Camden I was told that the Camden and Atlantic Railroad had been completed only as far as Spring Garden. I traveled that far on a freight train, and at Spring Garden I took a stage. We stopped at Baker's Hotel, in May's Landing, and got to Absecon the following evening at seven o'clock.... There was a small steamboat running [to] Atlantic City, but when we arrived at evening, the captain said it was too late for him to make the trip. But there were several of us bound for Atlantic, so we finally persuaded him to take us.... The city was then a waste of sand hills, ponds, and cedars. I remained there a week and then went back to Philadelphia. When the United States Hotel was being built I came back, and have remained ever since. But if anyone had told me during my first visit that Atlantic City would some day become my home, I would have laughed heartily at the absurdity.

While the town's fledgling hotel industry was a direct result, indeed a subsidiary, of the new railway, the earliest inn belonged to Aunt Millie Leeds, Jeremiah's

HARPER'S WEEKLY.

JOURNAL OF CIVILIZATION.

Vol. XXXIV. No. 1755
Copyright, 1890 by Harper & Brothers
All Rights Reserved

NEW YORK, SATURDAY, AUGUST 9, 1890

TEN CENTS A COPY.
INCLUDING SUPPLEMENT.

By 1890 the resort was known internationally as a place to relax and recuperate. Note that the woman in the center sits in a wheelchair, precursor to the famed Boardwalk rolling chair.

widow, who received a license to operate a tavern in 1839, the year after her husband's death. "When the railroad did come," according to a turn-of-the-century history, "half a dozen houses larger than the old Leeds homestead came into existence, also the pretentious United States Hotel, the still larger Surf House, the Mansion and Congress Hall, which dispensed hospitality to visiting thousands."

And, in fact, a tourist boom occurred within months of the last tap on the golden spike. On soil that once couldn't raise a tomato, wood-frame buildings sprouted, including by 1857 three churches, a lighthouse, a market house, and numerous railroad structures. It was estimated that in 1860, when Atlantic City had a permanent population of around seven hundred, as many as four thousand tourists could be housed and fed at any one time: four hundred or so at hotels

Atlantic City was touted as a place that could cure all ills. Notices from the nineteenth century promised fast relief for everything from consumption to insanity.

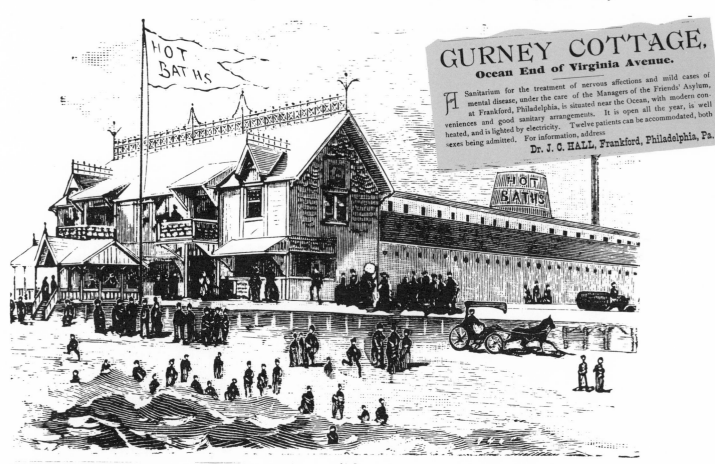

GURNEY COTTAGE,
Ocean End of Virginia Avenue.

A Sanitarium for the treatment of nervous affections and mild cases of mental disease, under the care of the Managers of the Friends' Asylum, at Frankford, Philadelphia, is situated near the Ocean, with modern conveniences and good sanitary arrangements. It is open all the year, is well heated, and is lighted by electricity. Twelve patients can be accommodated, both sexes being admitted. For information, address
Dr. J. C. HALL, Frankford, Philadelphia, Pa.

KIPPLE & McCANN'S
◉ HOT BATHS. ◉

such as the United States and the Surf House, twenty-five or less at rooming houses such as the Girard Saloon and Odd Fellows'. In just two years man and machine had done more to change the face of Absecon Island than had centuries of ripping winds and unrelenting tides.

The locomotive wasn't the only machine luring thousands to Atlantic City. The publicity machine was running full blast, telling of a place that had the most amazing effects on the body and mind. Conveniently omitting mention of the winds from the east, the greenhead flies, or the mosquitoes, the machine spun a tale that "even in mid-winter, when the Northern world is housed up in overheated quarters...sojourners in Atlantic City are lolling on the sands, reveling in glorious sunlight, and drinking in deep droughts of strength-creating air."

Yes, Atlantic City could cure your ills. "Pneumonia and bronchitis are of infrequent origin here," wrote Dr. Lewis Reed, the town's first resident physician. "I have not known an uncomplicated attack of either disease to prove fatal." The air, they said, was rich in ozone, and if you suffered from consumption, catarrh, asthma, rheumatism, cardiac dropsy, colds, laryngitis, pneumonia, Bright's disease, diabetes, eczema, digestive disorders, neurasthenia, insanity, or all of the above, come on down!

The city provided junkets to out-of-town doctors, as Atlantic City threatened to become America's capital of quackery. By 1900 and beyond, the healing powers of the place were accepted scientific truths, as expressed in the sober treatise of (the curiously named) Dr. M. D. Youngman:

> The diseases in which benefit is derived by a residence at Atlantic City are manifold, and a recitation of them would read much like the label of a popular proprietary medicine.... I would mention firstly the large class of neurasthenics, cases of nervous prostration, etc.; these are mostly mixed up in some way with faulty elimination, although as to which is cause and which is effect is a mooted point. Anyway, the regular and restful life, the strong, bracing air, the greatly improved sleeping at night, the superior facilities for carrying out the rest come in appropriate instances and administering various baths.

BY THE EIGHTIES, Atlantic City had evolved past the embryo stage and was already taking on the appearance, even the personality, of the mature beast. As the Camden and Atlantic Railroad continued to pump life, i.e., Philadelphia tourists, into the young city, competitive railways were built to enhance the flow.

The most notable of these was the Narrow-Gauge line, conceived and constructed by disaffected executives of the C and A. John F. Hall, in *The Daily Union History of Atlantic City and County* (1900), reported that "a few capitalists who had thoroughly investigated the costs and prospects...at once subscribed to a sufficient amount of stock to secure [the Narrow-Gauge's] completion." And no wonder: the Camden and Atlantic cost forty-thousand dollars a mile to build, while the new line was expected to cost a third of that. It wound up costing even less. The entire route was built in ninety days, and the first Narrow-Gauge locomotive chugged into Atlantic City on July 7, 1877.

Competition between the lines resulted in a dramatic boost to tourism. Round-trip tickets from Philadelphia, formerly $3.00, were reduced to $1.25. Weekend crowds grew so great that supplies of meat, milk, and bread were at times entirely exhausted in Atlantic City. Few failed to see it: Atlantic City was out of the woods and on a crash course to prosperity. The joyride would last for more than half the next century.

Not that there weren't casualties. The laborers who hammered down the tracks, and built the early hotels, were, for the most part, poor and black, drawn from the South by the promise of work. The first to settle permanently was Billy Bright, who lived in a shanty on Rhode Island Avenue. Others followed quickly. From 1870 to 1885, 1,220 blacks made permanent homes in Atlantic City, 15 percent of the town's population. By 1905, Atlantic City was 20 percent black, five years later, 25 percent.

Since employment at the resort was mainly seasonal, much of the black work

The first Camden and Atlantic Railroad trains consisted of three cars and a wood-burning locomotive. Passengers sat on bare boards, plagued by smoke and mosquitoes. Inset, Reading Railroad advertisement, circa 1906.

ATLANTIC CITY

Scale 400 ft. to one inch

1877.

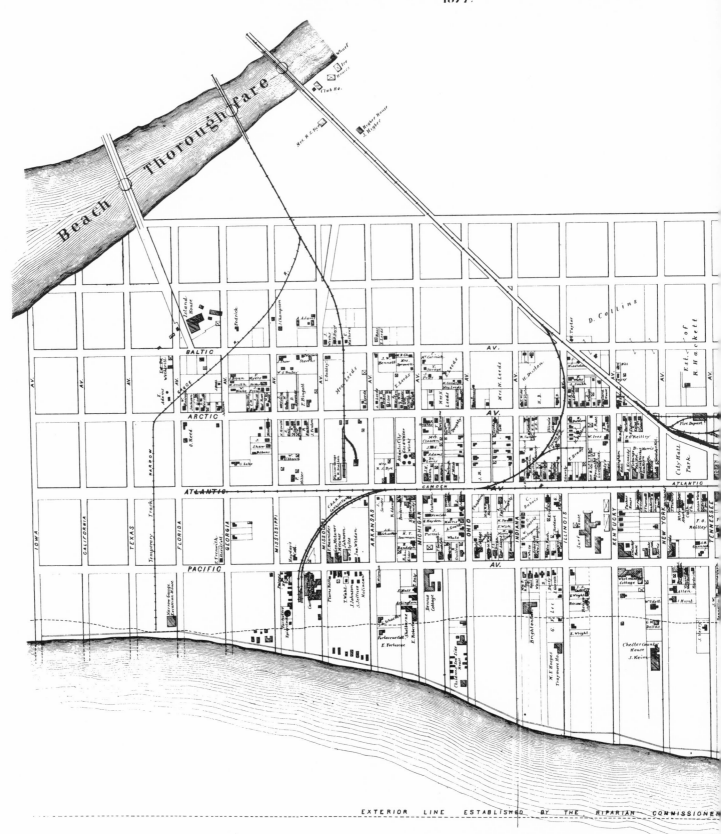

EXTERIOR LINE ESTABLISHED BY THE RIPARIAN COMMISSIONER

A T L A N T I C

force was without income part of the year. The trumpet that blared about Atlantic City's healthgiving air was silent about the mortality rate in the black section of town. It was staggering. Alfred Heston, the city's chief propagandist at the turn of the century, tried to shrug off the issue: "Colored people come here for the purpose of doing laundry work and waiting, and their children are bottle-fed and neglected. The mortality is therefore very great among them."

Charles E. Funnell, in his excellent social history, *By the Beautiful Sea* (1975), observed that the cheap black labor force was chiefly responsible for the speed with which Atlantic City evolved. In a hundred years the great-grandchildren of that work force would be blamed for the city's near-fatal decline. For the time being, however, the resort had more than enough hands to make its beds, wash its dishes, lay its bricks, tote its valises.

On the other side of the tracks, Atlantic City was giving rise to its first generation of self-made men, shrewd businessmen who seized the time and squeezed hard. One such was Joseph Fralinger, a jack-of-all-trades from Philadelphia who came to the shore hoping its magical air would cure his ailing wife. Fralinger, who

was born in 1848, saw "the possibilities in catering to the tastes of visitors who were beginning to flock to the local beaches," and set up fruit and candy stands along the strand. In no time at all, Fralinger, a community leader as well as an entrepreneur, was wheeling and dealing real estate, erecting theaters, and establishing an empire of saltwater taffy that would become "Famous the World Over." Fralinger, in fact, invented neither the candy nor the saline gimmick. Like so many who made fortunes in Atlantic City, he merely capitalized on the moment better than others.

Stories vary about the origin of saltwater taffy, though most give credit to David Bradley. One night in 1883, goes a popular saga, Bradley's taffy stand was swamped by a storm. When a child approached the stand the next morning and asked for taffy, Bradley replied sadly, "You mean *saltwater* taffy, don't you?" Local historians would have us believe that the news spread up and down the beach, causing scores of customers to assemble at Bradley's counter. Whatever the case, saltwater taffy and Atlantic City were soon synonymous. The rest is cavities.

Along with success came frustration, as entrepreneurs and impresarios fell over themselves to cash in on the surge. In 1881, Colonel George Howard revealed

The candy that ate Atlantic City—saltwater taffy was first sold in 1883, six pieces for a nickel. Joseph Fralinger, the town's biggest name in chewing, entered the field three years later with molasses, then vanilla and chocolate. Here are views of two taffy emporiums—Fralingers's and James'—from before and after the turn of the century.

Victorian design marked the Atlantic City of the 1890s. The Fish House, a social club, is an interesting example. A historian of the early resort characterized its Victorianism as "urban vigor and squalor, florid but charming sentimentality, optimism and bad taste, ingenuity and eccentricity."

Open-air trolleys shuttled sightseers to neighboring communities. 1890.

plans to erect Atlantic City's first amusement pier. A year later, as fireworks exploded over the sea, a 650-foot wooden promenade—set upon inadequate pilings—was opened to the public. Within a month or two, the whole business was washed away in a tempest. Howard returned the next season with a new pier, this one two hundred feet longer than the first. Less than a year thereafter, in January 1884, a ship called the *Robert Morgan* sailed into the ballroom, dashing the pier and Colonel Howard's hopes. Others would succeed where Howard failed.

A mere thirty years following Atlantic City's birth, ocean madness was as much a part of the air as the ozone. On a wooden esplanade built over the beach, vendors hawked the most bizarre goods and services. Mechanical marvels turned riders' stomachs upside down, and an iron spider, as tall as a building, ambled across the sea, as we shall learn. Concerts on the sand were held every evening, as well as gala dances in the hotel ballrooms. By 1900, *anything* was possible on Absecon Island. A headline in the *Philadelphia Inquirer:*

HALF AN HOUR IT WILL TAKE TO REACH ATLANTIC CITY

NEW SYSTEM OF TRANSIT PROMISED BY COMBINATION OF CAPITALISTS BY WHICH PHILADELPHIANS MAY BE WHIRLED TO THE SEA IN THIRTY MINUTES

The accompanying illustration was a scene from tomorrowland: an aluminum, bullet-shaped monorail speeding coastward. Owing to realities too numerous to mention, Lina Beecher's monorail never got built.

Atlantic City's personality was complete and, as shrewd observers have noted, that personality was gloriously split. On the one hand, Atlantic City was wholesome, offering sunshine and surf, even new hope for the terminally ill. On the other hand, Atlantic City was crazy as a gull, a festival of midways and monorails, and God-knows-what-next. As James Huneker wrote in *New Cosmopolis* (1915): "Atlantic City is not a treat for the introspective. It is all on the surface; it is hard, glittering, unspeakably cacophonous, and it never sleeps at all. Three days and you crave the comparative solitude of Broadway and Thirty-fourth Street; a week and you may die of insomnia."

Had everything happened just a little too fast? Would the weight of the trains, the hotels, the piers, the crowds, cause Absecon Island to sink, to disappear forever in a timeless sea? A few lonely voices argued so, but Atlantic City's smart money was betting on the contrary. The town that Budd, Leeds, Pitney, and Osborne built had come too far to turn back now—there were too many people depending on it. As Bruce Bliven proclaimed in the *New Republic*, December 29, 1920: "When Americans dream of that perfect society which is some day to be, what form does that imagining take? Atlantic City, New Jersey."

Why, it was as plain as the sand in your shoes.

A girl and her sand castles.

SAND CASTLES

Like the bathing beauty she was, Atlantic City tiptoed down to the water's edge, looking saucy. For her, the sea was a stage set, little more than a lovely backdrop. Dressed up in a multitude of costumes, she strutted and posed against it, entertaining her audiences, showing her stuff. She was tempting, reckless, unpredictable, flamboyant, vulgar, and boy, was she built!

You have the impression she never liked getting her feet wet, this beauty, wasn't the kind who tracked in sand. At night, when the ocean turned purple, then black, she slipped into something more glittery, something a *lady* would wear.

Enter—modestly at first—the Boardwalk. It was put down to keep the sand off the hotel carpets, but it quickly became Atlantic City's "medley of life...the frantic rush and indescribable gabble of a Babel-like chorus, the dazzling single line of booths, stores, divans, holes-in-the-wall hotels, cafés, carousels, soda-fountains, shows; the buzzing of children, the appeals of fakers, the quick glance of her eye."

The urge to be florid was understandably great. As James Huneker continued in *New Cosmopolis:*

> In the foreground a brilliant sea...as a background against a western sky-line is set a row of hotels, some palaces, some breath-catching, many commonplace. And the piers—the Steel Pier, the Auditorium, Young's, Heinz's, and the new million-dollar steel-and-concrete pier of John Young, completed sometime; another Atlantic City, on steel and iron stilts extending a half-mile into the water, containing a half-hundred diversions.

The Boardwalk! It wasn't always Atlantic City's answer to Piccadilly Circus, the Champs Elysées, Times Square on New Year's Eve. It was a solution to a headache, a way to keep the goddamn sand off the rugs, and off the seats of the Camden and Atlantic's passenger cars. Alexander Boardman, a railroad conductor, and Jacob Keim, proprietor of the Chester County Hotel, were fed up. On April 1, 1870, they petitioned the city council, asking that a footwalk be established along a suitable stretch of the beachfront.

A month later the council resolved:

> That the city build a board walk from Congress Hall (Massachusetts and Pacific) to the Excursion House (between Missouri and Mississippi). That said walk be 10 feet wide; that boards be laid lengthwise; that the Committee be instructed to proceed with the erection of the walk immediately; that the Ordinance Committee be instructed to draft an ordinance prohibiting erection of any bathhouse or shanty of any kind within 30 feet of the walk; and none on the ocean side except by permission of Council.

The fabled Boardwalk became higher, wider, and longer in five stages. The first (top) was in 1870, when twelve-foot sections were set down on the beach to keep sand out of visitors' shoes. At summer's end the boards were carted off and stored. The second Boardwalk, 1880, was fourteen feet wide, also a temporary structure. The third walk (center), 1884, was a permanent esplanade twenty feet wide, two miles long. Then came the fourth (bottom), 1890, the first with railings along the sides.

The mile-long promenade, which cost five-thousand dollars, was dedicated on June 16, 1870. According to Frank Butler's *Book of the Boardwalk* (1953), its beams were "one and one-half inches thick, nailed to joists set crosswise, two feet apart, built in sections, said to have been twelve feet long, so that these sections could be taken up and moved from the reach of storm tides. They were laid on rows of posts, set alternately two and three across the width, and two feet apart in length, projecting about ten inches above the sand." At season's end, and for seasons to come, the Boardwalk was taken apart and stored for the winter.

By 1880, thousands of strollers had splintered the walkway, and a new wooden path, four feet wider and somewhat longer, was set down in its place. Bowing to pressure from merchants and innkeepers, the city council allowed commerce to creep closer. Be it resolved: that buildings may be erected to within ten feet of the walk, all except bathhouses, which had to maintain a discreet distance of fifteen feet.

Three years later the revised ordinance was trampled by business leaders. Butler notes that in the city directory of 1883, nearly one hundred enterprises had

The fifth and present Boardwalk, forty feet wide, four miles long, was finished in 1896.

By the early 1900s the Boardwalk had developed a reputation—it was sexy.

permanent Boardwalk addresses, in addition to the numerous stalls and stands. But the planks on the sand were flimsy; an 1884 storm destroyed the modest walkway and virtually everything along it. The subsequent version was set on pilings five feet above the beach, so that tides could wash safely beneath. Still, there were no railings along the boards and accidents occurred. One contemporary account told of a day the walk caved in as twenty-five visitors stood "watching beer garden waitresses and female performers bathe." Another grave report said that "nearly every day somebody falls off the Boardwalk. In almost every instance the parties have been flirting."

Providence signaled its disapproval on September 9, 1889, when a hurricane wrecked the Boardwalk, nearly washing away in one swoop the waitresses and the wolves. The city fathers fought back. By the following spring, a new and improved fourth Boardwalk appeared, twenty-four feet wide, ten feet high, nearly four miles long. Neither God nor man could take *this* baby away, a permanent structure with railings on both sides.

While town officials permitted no buildings on the ocean side, the other side was chuggy-jammed with attractions. A stroller in 1900 wrote that the "booths run the gamut from home missions to vaudeville; from oysters to photographers. They also include book stalls, sun parlors, Japanese stalls—outside of which a

Wall-to-wall commerce on the Boardwalk, circa 1912.

Right, *Boardwalk people-watchers, or "railroads," circa 1900. Below, "No snow on the Boardwalk!" the Chamber of Commerce boasted year after year. No such claim was heard on Easter Sunday, 1915.*

Above, *Boardwalk fast food, circa 1925.* Left, *"Loop the Loop," an early Boardwalk amusement, 1901.*

23

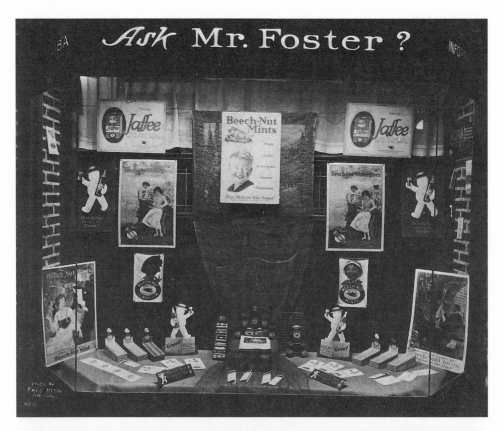

Boardwalk shop windows, circa 1928.

Gypsies have been living in Atlantic City since 1869, their presence visible in the fortune-tellers' booths along the walk. This one is from the thirties.

crowd is usually gathered watching the persevering Japs paint flower panels at fifty cents each—and fortune tellers, who invariably prophesy wealth and a large family at a reasonable fee of fifty cents. And there, almost bordering on this gingerbread, clapboard creation of man, is the sea—its surf sparkling in the sun as if smiling to itself at the thought that with one sweep of its long, green arm it would wipe the beach clear."

Why, you could fall in love with this place! Why, you could even fall in love with love! Americans listened to popular songs inspired by the scene, as the Boardwalk developed a reputation—it was sexy. One of the earliest hits was "Moonlight on the Boardwalk":

> *Honey, you make me do what you know I oughtn't to.*
> *Oh, when it is moonlight, down on the*
>   *Boardwalk,*
> *My dearie, that's where I'll be,*
> *... And every time it's moonlight, then it's spoon-light,*
> *Honey, wait for me.*

The Boardwalk had replaced the ocean as Atlantic City's greatest attraction. There were so many walkers walking, rolling chairs rolling, lovers loving, that an expanded fifth Boardwalk was decreed in 1896, which, given some minor fixings, is the Boardwalk of today. (The familiar herringbone pattern of the boards dates from 1916.)

Designed and constructed by the Phoenix Bridge Company, this Boardwalk

Heinz Pier, "Crystal Palace
by the Sea," where free pickles
were given away for forty-six
years. The pier was destroyed
by a hurricane in 1944.

QUALITY IS TO A PRODUCT WH

VINEGAR BEANS PICKLES

was supported by steel pilings and girders forty feet wide and ran slightly over four miles. Among its other virtues, it was the artery that physically divided the two sides of the town's personality. On one side the walk was lined with fabled hotels, which offered refuge from the ambulating chaos below: ocean views, restful sleep, saltwater baths, hearty meals. Jutting forth from the walk's other side were the amusements piers: gaudy, raucous, bejeweled at night.

James R. Applegate, learning from Colonel Howard's mistakes, opened the first successful amusements pier in 1884—a multidecked, 625-foot-long construction at the foot of Tennessee Avenue. Even though Applegate, a Boardwalk photographer, booked concerts and vaudeville there, the pier never approached the hurly-burly of its later cousins. More than anything else, Applegate's devoted itself to health and contentment: picnic areas, sunbathing pavilions, a parking lot for baby carriages, and the most talked-about feature, a huge ice-water fountain that used up three-thousand pounds of ice a day. At Applegate's Pier, all men could refresh themselves, as suggested by its advertising jingle:

Four spacious decks high in the air,
The old, the young, the millionaire,
The worthy poor as well,
Seek health and rest, all find the same,
Shielded from the sun as well as rain,
A paradise to dwell.

The Glass Pavilion (above) was at the outer end of Heinz Pier. On its roof was the seventy-foot-high 57 varieties sign. Pickle products were displayed inside, next to marble busts of Socrates, Caesar, and Napoleon, among others.

After Applegate's came the Iron Pier (1886) at Massachusetts Avenue, notable for the fact that twelve years hence it became the Heinz Pier, purchased by H. J. himself to popularize his 57 varieties. That magic number glowed over the ocean for nearly fifty years, until the sign, and the pier underneath it, were destroyed in the hurricane of 1944. At the Heinz Pier there were free pickles, free pickle lapel pins, sundecks, and, later on, daily organ recitals.

The point was to promote pickles. George Prague, a citizen of Atlantic City since 1918, spoke for millions of children when he recalled: "The greatest thrill in the world was to go to the Heinz Pier. When you went in they gave you a little

Captain John Young's Million Dollar Pier, circa 1910. Inset, admission tickets to the pier. Right, the Cake Walkers, a dance troupe on Young's earlier Ocean Pier.

Inset above, *women ride a revolving disk at their own risk. The deep-sea net haul (right) at Million Dollar Pier was held twice daily, yielding all varieties of fish, shellfish, and even an occasional tire.*

Steel Pier (bottom), "Showplace of the Nation," was the most widely known of all the Boardwalk piers, stretching 1,780 feet into the ocean. Right, a Boardwalk entrance to Steel Pier, circa 1936. Center, performers from the water circus, circa 1935.

George C. Tilyou's Steeplechase Pier was the self-described "Funny Place." Opened in 1904, it rented out clown costumes for tourists to wear on amusements such as the Whirlpool (left) and the Whip (below).

pin with a Heinz pickle on it. And they also gave you pickles. The one you could wear was good, but boy, the one you could eat was *terrific.*"

H. J. was ever a salesman, never a showman. Captain John Lake Young, though—now, *there* was a showman. In 1891, Young and business partner Stewart McShay, already bathhouse and merry-go-round moguls, purchased Applegate's quay and turned it into the granddaddy of Atlantic City's madcap Boardwalk piers. Young, who loved seafood as he loved life itself, instituted the famous daily nethaul, which he supervised personally. Visitors strained to see what ungodly creatures would be yanked from the deep. Young also opened a dance ballroom, installed the latest rides and midway games, scheduled vaudeville acts and concerts. A hoofer named Dora Johnson introduced a dance that made Young's Ocean Pier the "Home of the Cakewalk." He imported Sarah Bernhardt for her first Atlantic City appearance. And it all paid off: Young's Ocean Pier bustled until fire destroyed it in 1912. In the meantime, the captain had added a second, even more elaborate, toy to his empire.

Young's Million Dollar Pier opened in 1906 and soon became symbolic of Atlantic

The rooftop solarium at the genteel Craig Hall, a turn-of-the-century hotel operated by ardent prohibitionists.

City's unquenchable thirst for entertainment. Harry Houdini appeared (and disappeared), to the astonishment of thousands. Bull Moose candidate Teddy Roosevelt gave a speech on the pier in 1912, to crowds so thick a car in his party ran over, and killed, a potential vote. Early Miss Americas were crowned on Million Dollar Pier, and there were movies, conventions, and exhibits of every description. The cherry on top was Captain Young's home, a Grecian *cum* Venetian *cum* Elizabethan cottage at the tip of the pier, the world-famous No. 1 Atlantic Ocean, to be visited later on.

Piers sprang up all over. Down at Virginia Avenue, the Steel Pier, which would become the "Showplace of the Nation," opened in 1898. Then came Auditorium Pier, at Pennsylvania, later purchased by Coney Island impresario George C. Tilyou, who turned it into Steeplechase. Tilyou's extravaganza featured "the largest electric sign in the world," the Chesterfield sign, twenty-seven-thousand lightbulbs strong.

Late afternoon on the beach, circa 1948.

Grand hotels grew out of wood-framed guest cottages of the nineteenth century. The Dennis, a two-room summerhouse in 1860, expanded into a twenty-two-room guesthouse in 1867. It continued to grow further, as these pictures from 1901 to 1904 attest. The Dennis finally matured into a 550-room palace. Below right, the St. Dennis Room, circa 1930. Below left, an Atlantic City Thanksgiving, Hotel Dennis, 1935.

Above, *Hotel Dennis limousine, circa 1915.*

The Brighton Hotel, 1904, where guests sipped the renowned Brighton Punch. Ladies, for their own protection, were allowed just two glasses a day. Inset, circa 1946.

The year 1913 brought the Garden Pier, east of New Jersey Avenue, sedate by Young's and Tilyou's standards, with its formal flower beds leading to an open-air theater. Finally, there was Central Pier, on the site of Young's original pier, home of commercial exhibits, including a well-known model-homes display.

The piers, as we shall see, were more than places to amuse the kiddies. They were, in fact, some of the principal stages on which American show business developed—from minstrel revues to Broadway musicals, from vaudeville comedy to big bands, from the rise of the movies to riotous pop music. But they were ticky-tacky, these piers, and you always knew that, because they had to be repainted every season, the day would come when they'd be left to decay.

Ah, but you had a different feeling about the grand hotels that sternly overlooked the piers. Now, *these* were built to withstand the ages. Neither wind, nor rain, nor the latest fashion could erode the immortality of these places, these elegant bastions of manners. From the massive Traymore to the hulking brick skyscraper, the Claridge, the hotels were solid proof that Atlantic City was not built in a day, nor could it ever crumble that quickly.

The biggest, most glamorous of the early hotels was the six-hundred-room United States, for a while the largest in the nation, constructed by the Camden and Atlantic Railroad in 1854. Unlike many of the resort's renowned hotels—which expanded from initially modest structures—the United States was a giant from the start: four stories high, occupying the entire block bounded by Atlantic, Pacific,

Completed in 1930, the Claridge, twenty stories proud, was the last of the great old hotels to be built near the Boardwalk.

Delaware, and Maryland Avenues. There were gardens, sun porches, rooms furnished in walnut, and mule trains to cart guests to the beach. The hotel prospered despite several changes in ownership. Then in the early 1890s, the United States was irreparably harmed by a good old-fashioned insect swarm. William McMahon, in his *So Young…So Gay!* (1970), reported that clouds of mosquitoes dive-bombed the grounds, causing a stampede of horses, carriage wrecks, and blazing bonfires. The publicity so damaged the hotel that it never reclaimed its former glory.

The nineteenth century gave rise to most of the other famous hotels, some of which glittered then faded, others of which recharged themselves, managing to hang on. Among those to disappear early were the McGlade and the Garden. The former was one of the most opulent, though it finally expired due to its distance from the Boardwalk. The Garden Hotel, built in 1897, was an unheard-of seven stories, serving as a most exclusive retreat for the socially prominent friends of its owner, Philadelphian John Weyth.

Another turn-of-the-century marvel was the Hotel Rudolf, with its "balconies, bedrooms, and diningroom overlooking the sea." According to a contemporary source, the Rudolf housed a "spacious ball-room, parlor, and music room [that] adjoin the office and exchange, which is furnished with Holland and French designs and on the polished floors Oriental rugs of great beauty are noticed. To insure pure water an artesian well has been sunk on the premises."

Left, *the Merry-Go-Round* bar *at the Ritz-Carlton.* Right, *the Nautical Room, Wiltshire Hotel, 1938. An ensemble called the Musical Middies occupies the bandstand.* Inset, *actress Irene Rich wields the champagne, 1937.*

A room at the Rudolf cost five dollars in 1900, the going rate for the top ten hotels in town. If you didn't mind taking a step down, a place like the Galen Hall, Kenilworth, or Berkeley would run about three. The Ponce de León, Rovere, and Norwood were a dollar less; and then there were the many rooming houses near the beach, where a dollar would get you a bed and not much more.

Three generations of vacationers, conventioneers, honeymooners, and even soldiers are more familiar with the other great hotels that date from 1900 and before: the Dennis, the Traymore, the Marlborough-Blenheim, the Shelburne, the Brighton, the Chelsea. Then there were the sizable newer hotels: the Ritz-Carlton, the President, the Ambassador, the Claridge. Each in its heyday buzzed with excitement, its ballroom a swirl of music and dancing, its barroom a jangle of conversation and cheer.

Many started out as cracker boxes. In 1879, the Traymore was but a small wooden cottage named, says William McMahon, in honor of a frequent guest, "Uncle" Al Harvey, who spoke incessantly of his Maryland estate, Traymore, which in turn was named for his Irish birthplace. Following a series of expansions and improvements, the Traymore that history remembers—then later condemned—was the building completed in 1915, in accordance with the awesome design of William L. Price.

Not far down the walk was the Marlborough-Blenheim, which grew from guesthouse simplicity into the first Atlantic City hotel to offer hot and cold running saltwater. In 1906, when it was rebuilt, it became the first hotel in the world to

Left, *Abbott (the one with the celery in his eye) and Costello having dinner at the Hotel Roma, a family-run guesthouse.* Below right, *the Hotel Apollo, 1926, a small celebration of Art Deco that catered to visiting entertainers.* Below left, *the staff of the Fox Manor, an off-Boardwalk hotel that specialized in the honeymoon trade, 1947.*

Praised for its Boardwalk façade, the Blenheim (opposite page) *was constructed with reinforced concrete in 1906. Thomas Edison, who owned the cement company, often visited the project.* Upper left, *the Wedgewood Room at the Marlborough-Blenheim, where a parachutist, jumping from a balloon, accidentally fell through the dome in the early 1900s.* Upper right, *one of the lobbies of the Marlborough-Blenheim. In 1979, despite protests, the landmark was demolished by casino operators.*

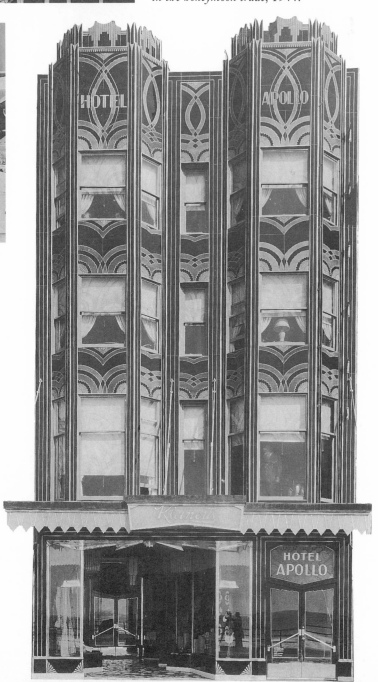

A Holiday Meal at the Breakers

106 The Breakers. Atlantic City, N. J.

Mrs. Herman Silverman, who has spent fifty-seven summers in Atlantic City, and who now lives in Ventnor, a neighboring community, recalls some festivities.

At the Breakers Hotel, God, did they give you food! First of all, the place was very, very spacious. They'd give you a beautiful holiday meal.... From soup to nuts! With wine, gefilte fish, and soup with knaidlach, roast chicken, knishes, candied sweet potatoes, and all kinds of goodies.

There wasn't a thing missing from that meal. And you could eat as many portions—God, if you were a big eater—there were people eating two or three portions of their main platter....

And everything was homemade. The rolls were hot, and the cookies were homemade, and such pastries....They'd have sour cream, and they'd have all kinds of fishes—lox, and smoked fish. What didn't they have! If you went there for a week you had to put on fifteen pounds, I'm telling you! It was really beautiful!

COMING OF AGE ON THE BOARDWALK: six seasons in the life of a young visitor to Atlantic City.

be constructed of reinforced concrete, the pouring of which was supervised by the developer of the process, Thomas Edison.

Classier still was the Brighton, which didn't think twice about turning you away if it didn't like your looks—or, at one time, if you had the audacity to arrive in an automobile. The Brighton was the summer home of Colonel Anthony J. Drexel Biddle who, among his other accomplishments, once threw a glass of Brighton Punch at a streetcar conductor.

Much has been made of the Brighton Punch, a mystical concoction highly praised by such experts as Ulysses S. Grant, Lillian Russell, and Diamond Jim Brady. Served in the lounge in the early evening, the secret recipe was as closely guarded as Coca-Cola's. Owing to its potency, ladies were allowed only two glasses a day, and even the most experienced, two-fisted males were said to totter helplessly after

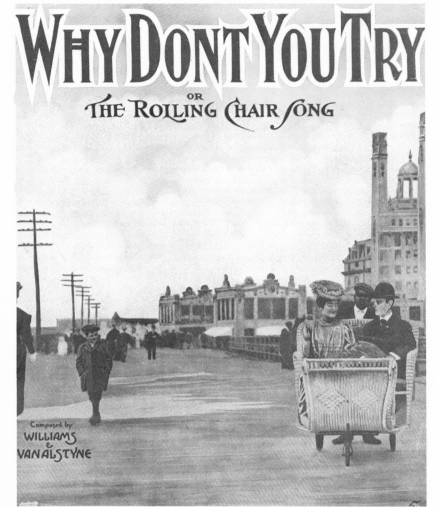

three. A former bellhop at the Brighton insists that no one has ever learned the exact formula for the brew. Nevertheless, a close approximation follows:

> 1 ½ oz. rye (100-proof)
> 1 oz. dark rum
> 1 tsp. brown sugar
> Juice of half a lemon
> *Shake with cracked ice fifteen times.*
> *Pour into a tall glass and add a*
> *half-slice of orange.*

Popular and powerful figures of the times lent their auras to the great hotels. Longtime boss of the Atlantic City political machine, Enoch "Nucky" Johnson, dispensed favors from his digs at the Ritz. Paul Whiteman and his Rhythm Boys (including Bing Crosby) added zest to the Ambassador. The twenty-story Claridge was Frank Sinatra's Atlantic City home, as well as other show business giants of the forties.

Life in the hotels made Atlantic City one helluva town. Capone and Runyon just breezed in, and they're staying at the Ritz! Hey, did you hear? John L. Lewis blew his stack at the Chelsea and split from the A.F. of L.! Over at the Shelburne, Diamond Jim himself walked into the kitchen and, can you imagine?, made his own salad! And that gal from Philly, Princess Grace, the bricklayer's daughter, is lunching at the Claridge, a shrimp bowl no less!

In terms of design, the most striking hotel was the Marlborough-Blenheim, an amalgam of the Marlborough House, built in 1902, and the Blenheim, which opened its doors several years later. It was one of the first fireproof hotels in

Designs changed through the years, and by the late 1940s electric motors began to replace human chair pushers. Today, Boardwalk trams carry more riders than do individual chairs.

The beachfront in the late thirties. Boardwalk hotels, from left to right: *Shelburne, Dennis, Marlborough-Blenheim, Claridge, Traymore, Chalfonte-Haddon Hall.*

It took thirty-six years for the Traymore to evolve (these pages) *from a modest boardinghouse to a massive hotel.*

Atlantic City, and the first to have a private bath in every room. The architect was William L. Price of Philadelphia, and the style—well, it was breathtaking. Huneker wrote in *New Cosmopolis:*

> The architecture of one section is so extraordinary that I gasped when I saw it. I haven't the remotest notion of the architect's name, nor did I go into the hotel, fearing the usual perfection of modern appliances and all the rest of the useful things that are driving romance away for all ages. It was the exterior that glued my feet to the Boardwalk. If Coleridge, in Kubla Khan, or Poe, in The Doman of Arnheim, had described such a fantastic structure, we should have understood, for they are men of imagination....The architecture might be Byzantine. It suggests St. Marco's at Venice, St. Sophia at Constantinople, or a Hindu Palace, with its crouching dome, its operatic facade, and its two dominating monoliths with blunt tops. Built of concrete, the exterior is a luxurious exfoliation in hues, turquoise and fawn. I did not venture near the building for fear some Atlantic City Flip would cry out: "Wake up! You are at Winslow Junction!" If I ever go to [Atlantic City] again it will be to see this dream architecture, with its strange evocation of Asiatic colour and music.

To sightsee the great hotels along the Boardwalk, you had two choices of transport: your feet, or, much more happily, a rolling chair. The wheeled seats that Atlantic City made famous were actually imported from the Philadelphia Centennial of 1876.

They rolled to the shore several years later, thanks to a hardware store operator named William Hayday, who thought to rent them to invalids. These "temples of contentment," "citadels of restful travel," were soon favored Boardwalk vehicles for everyone—the healthy as well as the infirm. The boom came when Harry Shill brought out two- and then three-seater models in the early 1880s. Shill, himself a cripple, designed graceful wicker chairs with sloping, swanlike necks.

A ride in a rolling chair was bewitching, like a carriage ride through Central Park, or a gondola tour of the Venetian canals. All three conveyances are built not for speed, but for romance. In 1905, "Why Don't You Try," or "The Rolling Chair Song," was hummed up and down the beach:

> *Did you ever see a maiden in a little rolling chair,*
> *Room for two, Sue and you*
> *Hear the salty breezes through her curly locks of hair,*
> *Oceans blue, so are you*
> *For another lucky fellow is attending by her side,*
> *There to stay, if he may*
> *And she whispers in his ear,*
> *"Don't be so distant dear,*
> *Tho' we first met yesterday."*

One hopes the song had nothing to do with the fact that rolling chairs were banned later that year. Officials groused that there were too many of the damn

It took, on April 27, 1972, less than ten seconds to blow it up.

things, and that the Boardwalk was not built to accommodate them. But the chairs rolled again after a few seasons, their numbers now regulated by law, and their rides considerably smoother given the new longitudinally laid boards set into the walk.

You didn't have to be rich to hire a rolling chair; hell, you felt like a million to be aglide in one. A writer in the *New Republic*, 1920, explained: "We ride in wheeled chairs…as a sensual experience, not from infirmity. Indeed, we sit erect with such an air of almost belligerent health as to prove we ride merely because we have the dollar."

The chairs rolled legends into the Boardwalk. George Noah, a retired manufacturer from Baltimore, rode the boards summer after summer, wearing a white turtleneck shirt with a message stitched across the front: GEORGE—THE WORKING GIRL'S FRIEND. Henry Ford, a frequent roller in the twenties, was shunned by the wiser chair pushers. In their words, Ford was a "flat," a lousy tipper. Day after day, he'd tip you a dime, saying, "Now, save that." As for Diamond Jim Brady, he was the highest roller of all, never tipping less than a ten-spot, even for the shortest of spins.

In the late 1940s—as Americans grew enamored of push-button living, manmade fibers, and artificial everything—rolling chairs with electric motors were introduced on the Boardwalk. There was hardly a ripple of protest. And why should there have been? At Atlantic City, like everywhere, times change. In a few more years, even the giant hotels would tumble or close, replaced by motor courts with names like Malibu, Deauville, Monte Carlo, not to mention Howard Johnson and the Holiday Inn.

Gone were the Brighton, the Traymore, the Chelsea, the St. Charles, the Breakers. Others remained, shadows of their former selves, converted into apartments, old-age homes, or limping along with humiliating vacancy rates. One of the last great buildings to be demolished was the Marlborough-Blenheim, the hotel that once glued your feet to the Boardwalk.

The reasons predate legalized gambling. Chief among them was the fact that visitors no longer came to Atlantic City by train, for two whole weeks or more, with a steamer trunk packed to the gills. They came in automobiles, for the weekend (if not just the day), with a T-shirt, bathing suit, and suntan lotion stuffed into the glove compartment.

That is, if they came to Atlantic City at all. As jet travel became accessible and cheap in the fifties, more and more vacationers went south, mainly to Miami Beach. Who needed Atlantic City's racial problems? Hello to Collins Avenue, goodbye to the grand old hotels.

Marvin Hume, a Boardwalk store owner for twenty-one years, remembers his thoughts as he watched the demolition of the Traymore on April 27, 1972:

> They had set a time of eight in the morning. I took two of my sons there. A strong wind was blowing out of the north at about twenty to thirty miles an hour, so they moved the lines back. Some people were on the beach. We stood there waiting…. Finally they gave the warning and detonated five large blasts…. The smoke and dust went into the air perhaps twelve or fifteen stories high, a tremendous mass…. It took only five or six seconds to have that building flat on the ground….
>
> It was really a memorable experience—we lost a very beautiful hotel.

The Absecon Lighthouse, built in 1857 at the urging of Dr. Jonathan Pitney, warned of treacherous inlet tides. It remains one of the resort's major landmarks.

Entertainer Paul Del Rio, nineteen inches high, celebrated his eighteenth birthday in 1938 on Million Dollar Pier.

BALLYHOO

THIS CHAPTER IS ABOUT AN ELEPHANT bigger than a house, a typewriter bigger than an elephant, and the largest light bulb ever lighted. It is about a man who sat on a flagpole, another who buried himself alive, and about two sisters who walked from Atlantic City to Miami. It is about the famous American singer who got his start by winning a dance contest, and about two couples who got married—one beneath the sea, the other in a dolphin tank. It is about how Ferris never invented the Ferris wheel, and about why the Wild Man of Borneo was arrested. It is about people who jumped out of balloons and helicopters, and from a high platform on horseback. It is about a man who ate more clams in an hour than you've eaten in a summer, and about hundreds of babies kept on public display as an attraction. This chapter is about what they've said Atlantic City is about: "Ocean, emotion, and constant promotion."

Once upon a time, there were those who tried to keep the lid on Atlantic City—at least on Sundays. Clergymen and God-fearing citizens were aghast that even on the Sabbath the merry-go-rounds turned, the minstrels strummed, and the novelty shops sold racy postcards. Now and again, a reformer railed against the sacrilege, supported in his rage by the editorial drumbeats of the Philadelphia dailies. Now and again, the governor of New Jersey got into the act, threatening martial law if the town didn't shape up.

Atlantic City turned a deaf ear. Sunday was the most popular day of the weekend at the resort, there being only four weekends to the month, just three months to the Season. And from the day of Creation, i.e., the day Atlantic City was born, the Season was everything. Let it be shouted so that even the heavens can hear: the business of Atlantic City is monkey business, Sundays included. Atlantic City was off on a race against sanity.

Consider the early amusements. In 1872, Isaac Newton Forrester erected his "Epicycloidal Diversion" on Mississippi Avenue. It was the earliest known version of what we now call (incorrectly) the Ferris wheel. Consisting of "four wheels, about 30 feet in diameter, resting on a circular platform, about 10 feet high," says *The Book of the Boardwalk*, it had a capacity of sixty-four persons, eight two-passenger cars to the wheel. The wheels turned up and down, but they also *turned sideways in a circle*, which meant you moved in twice as many directions as in a you-know-what-wheel.

Right, *the Hilton Sisters, Siamese-twin performers, 1933. Atlantic City was always big on natural oddities and was especially big on small people.* Below, *midget boxers, who fought in the Steel Pier Water Circus, circa 1935.*

Why, then, isn't the Ferris wheel the Forrester wheel? Why isn't, in fact, the Ferris wheel the Somers wheel? In 1892, Atlantic City's William Somers built a Boardwalk ride nearly identical to the one put up two years later by George Ferris at the Chicago Exposition. The only difference was that Ferris's was made of steel, while Somers' wheel was wood. Somers sued Ferris for patent infringement, but the latter died before the action was settled.

If history was unkind to overlook William Somers, it made amends by mercifully ignoring Reverend Ezra B. Lake. His "Ocean Tricyclemore Sea-Wagon," or "Sea Spider," rolled into the surf in 1890. It was a steam-powered derrick atop wheels, crowned by a wooden passenger deck. However amusing, it wasn't really an amusement; rather, Lake proposed the "Spider" as a device to aid drowning swimmers and shipwreck victims.

There were gears loose everywhere. One of the hottest attractions in the early nineties was the "Haunted Swing," which drew crowds at States and the Boardwalk. A large platform suspended over a furnished room gave riders the illusion of swinging back and forth at great speed. In fact, it was the *room* that moved, furniture and paintings being securely bolted to the walls and floor.

Atlantic City was also big on big people. Billed as "the world's largest twins," Billy and Benny McGuire hosted a 1977 event at which forty people tried to get into a giant T-shirt (119 inches wide at the shoulders).

Right, *Reverend Ezra B. Lake's "Ocean Tricylemore Sea-Wagon," or the "Sea Spider," 1890. The contraption was designed as a lifesaving vehicle, to rescue shipwreck victims and endangered bathers. Below, Isaac Newton Forrester's "Epicycloidal Diversion," an early (1872) version of what would become known as the Ferris wheel.*

An early amusement, 1894, the "Haunted Swing" gave twenty passengers an unforgettable ride for their money. The attraction was unique enough to be explained in Scientific American.

Contraptions such as these—together with ambitious "scenographs" that reenacted such catastrophies as the Johnstown Flood and Custer's Last Stand—represented the big deal stuff. Smaller bits of lunacy were found on almost every block of the Boardwalk. "We have...all kinds of catchpenny shows," read an 1880s hotel brochure. "The wonderful woman snake charmer, the man with the iron jaws, the learned pigs."

And coming soon: *incubated babies!*

A plaque at Missouri Avenue and the Boardwalk commemorated the notorious Premature Infant Exhibit of Dr. Martin A. Couney. From 1902 to 1943, Dr. Couney kept babies in glass display cases and lectured on the benefits of incubation. Couney claimed credit for inventing the incubator, and for saving the lives of fourteen thousand premature infants. Admission to the socially redeeming freak show was a quarter, "necessary because the tiny tots are given the very best medical care absolutely free." His lecture never failed to note that some of civilization's greatest figures were born prematurely, including Newton, Voltaire, Napoleon, and Darwin.

Included among the resort's
many daredevil acts was
Steel Pier's 1931 motorcycle
stunt. It featured a spinner
named CeDora, who roared
around a sixteen-foot globe
at seventy-five miles per
hour. Below, one hundred
feet atop Steel Pier, the Six
Hustreis performed high-
wire routines in 1931.

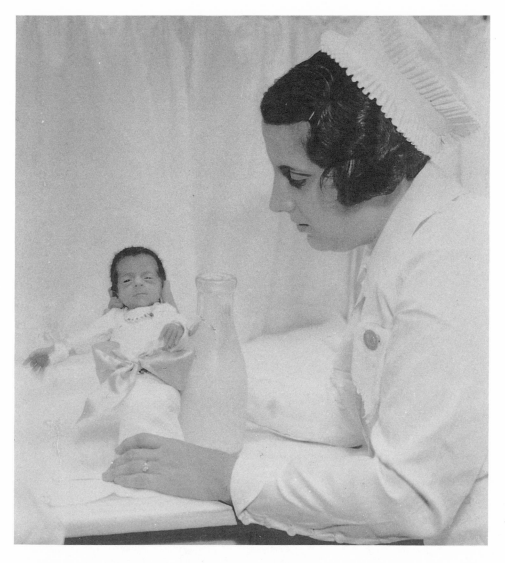

*A nurse displays a
featured attraction at the
incubated baby exhibit on
the Boardwalk.*

Atlantic City opened its arms to the show-off, the publicity hound, the daredevil.
The bigger the crowd you gathered, the more welcome you were. Stunts came in
all sizes, styles, and dangers.

There were stunts that you ate. In the 1890s three tourists competed in a gut-
heaving contest. The menu was oysters, sugar, pure soap, watermelon, and molasses.
The loser, that lucky fellow who sickened first, "set up a wine supper for the less dis-
tressed members of the party."

Fifty years later, Israel Weintraub, a three hundred-pound jitney driver, won the
eating contest at Atlantic City's Clam and Oyster Opening Tournament. "My
record is one hundred and forty-six clams in twenty minutes," he said. "This year
it's good I ain't hungry because I only need one hundred twenty to win."

There were stunts that took time. Alvin "Shipwreck" Kelly, who liked being called
"America's Luckiest Fool," broke his own flagpole-sitting record when he logged
forty-nine days on the Steel Pier in 1930. Kelly finally came down not because he
was bored, but because he missed his wife.

Ronald Harrison took a lower route in August 1952. The middle-aged Floridian buried himself in a glass-topped grave on Steel Pier, there to stay six weeks "in protest of present-day prices." Harrison, who made a living playing dead, consumed only liquids, and slept just four hours a night.

Some preferred to dance the time away. From May 26 to October 19, 1932, 101 couples competed in a dance marathon on Million Dollar Pier. At 8:20 the final morning it was down to Mary Fenton and Joie Ray, he a former Olympic sprinter, and Ruth Smith and Frank Lovecchio. Ray broke, sprinting once too often, this time to the men's room. That left Smith and Lovecchio to receive the applause of three thousand spectators. For Lovecchio it was only the beginning; in a few years he'd become nationally known as Frankie Laine. (Red Skelton was also involved in dance marathons—as an emcee at Convention Hall during the thirties.)

There were stunts that walked. A. F. Bergman, of Leetsdale, Pennsylvania, returned every year to Atlantic City, always on his birthday, May 14. Bergman's idea of a party was to walk as many miles as he was years old. In 1955, at seventy-one, he awoke before dawn and ate a modest breakfast. At six he started out from Captain Starn's Restaurant at the Inlet. At noon he reached his halfway point, thirty-six miles, finishing the full seventy-one at 8:57 P.M. At a news conference afterward,

Israel Weintraub (above), *a three hundred-pounder, won the 1945 national clam-eating tournament. Winning score: 120 clams. "A chewer don't have much of a chance," Weintraub said. "The gulpers have the best of it." Inset, Jay Tierney won the 1973 hot dog–eating competition. Winning score: nineteen hot dogs in five minutes.*

Alvin "Shipwreck" Kelly (opposite) *sat for forty-nine days on a thirteen-inch steel disk atop a flagpole on Steel Pier in 1930. In 1964 Dixie Blandy broke Kelly's mark by staying up seventy-eight days.*

63

Dance Marathon Champs

WINNERS in Atlantic City Boardwalk dance marathon, Frank Lovecchio, 23, Chicago, Ill., and Mrs. Ruth Smith, Lafayette, Ind., are shown at windup of event yesterday in which they danced more than 145 days, or 3501 hours. Mrs. Smith won last year's seashore marathon with Frank Miller, 37, Washington grandfather, a partner, after dancing 62 days.—(A. N. A.)

Above, *a scene from the Boardwalk marathon dance contest on Million Dollar Pier, 1932. Inset, the winning couple, Frankie (Laine) Lovecchio and Ruth Smith. Right, the "Atlantic City Hikers," as the press called them, Winifred (left) and Kathleen O'Malley, who walked 1,623 miles from the resort to Miami in 1922.*

Living corpse Ronald Harrison bid farewell to Dagmar as he prepared to spend forty-two days in a six-foot grave on Steel Pier (1952). Harrison was fed through a tube a secret "life-sustaining formula."

Bergman told reporters he had walked 300,000 miles in his lifetime. "Walking is healthy," he said, "if you don't overdo it."

If A. F. Bergman deserves commendation, double commendation goes to the O'Malley sisters, Kathleen, twenty-three, and Winifred, thirty-three, also known as the "Atlantic City Hikers." In 1922 they walked all the way from Atlantic City to Miami, leaving February 1, arriving September 18, covering every inch of the 1,623 miles on their own four feet. At post offices along the way, the O'Malley sisters picked up parcels of Atlantic City brochures and postcards, which they distributed as souvenirs. In a letter to the Atlantic City Chamber of Commerce, the sisters told of the many rides they were offered along the way. "I know they were given in a friendly spirit—others only to try us out. Your faith in us and our ambition to live up to that has enabled us to say 'no' when a ride looked very good. Don't forget the Atlantic City buttons. Your Atlantic City girls, Winifred and Kathleen O'Malley."

In 1948 Joseph Hackney jumped 145 feet from a blimp. In 1910 Walter Wellman lifted off from Atlantic City in the airship America (inset), hoping to be the first flyer to cross the ocean. A thousand miles out, heavy winds caused Wellman's crew to ditch. They were picked up at sea and returned to New York.

There were high flying stunts and stunts that fell to earth. Atlantic City holds a special place in this country's early aviation history. The term "airport" was coined at the resort, though who said it first is in question. Some tout Henry Woodhouse, an owner of the local airfield (later called Bader Field), while others advance William B. Dill, editor of the *Atlantic City Press* in 1919.

According to Frank Butler's Boardwalk history, an air carnival was held along the beach on July 2, 1910, at which Walter Brookins set a world's altitude record (6,175 feet), and Glenn H. Curtiss a fifty-mile speed record in one hour, fourteen minutes. The carnival also featured a demonstration of aerial bombing, as Curtiss

Stunts that went boom: The Flying Zachinis, headlined on Steel Pier, blasted themselves out of a cannon throughout the 1930s. Mlle. Alexme (inset), around the same time, was ordered by a judge to be shot out of a gun three times a day. The court had ruled on a contract dispute between Mlle. Alexme and the pier's management.

dropped oranges on a yacht, diving to within one hundred feet of its masts. A military man in the audience was impressed: "The trial shows absolutely that the day of the battleship for attack on foreign cities is nearing its end."

Three months after the show, Walter Wellman attempted an even more daring aerial act: he set out to cross the Atlantic in the dirigible *America*. Wellman managed to travel one thousand miles before heavy winds forced him to ditch. A steamship picked up the crew and returned them to New York. *America* was never recovered.

Two years later the crossing was tried again—by Melvin Vaniman, Wellman's mechanic. Vaniman lifted off in the airship *Akron*, but a couple of thousand feet

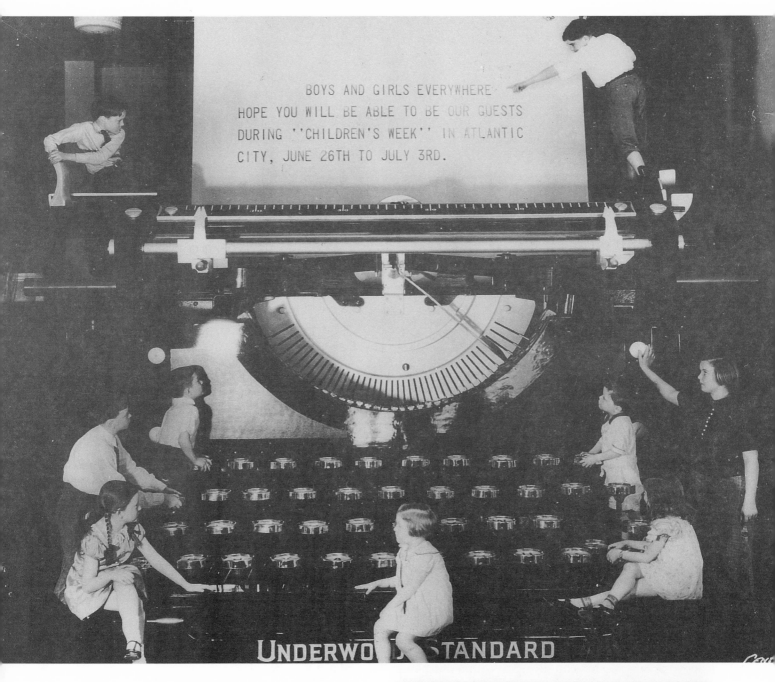

BOYS AND GIRLS EVERYWHERE
HOPE YOU WILL BE ABLE TO BE OUR GUESTS
DURING ''CHILDREN'S WEEK'' IN ATLANTIC
CITY, JUNE 26TH TO JULY 3RD.

UNDERWOOD STANDARD

Above, *Underwood's famed giant typewriter. The machine, displayed at Garden Pier and later at Convention Hall for twenty-two years, was turned into scrap during World War II. Women were always decorating something in Atlantic City. In 1954 (right) they decorated a make-believe cake to honor the town's centennial.*

The world's largest tire, courtesy of Goodyear, circa 1932.

above the city, the dirigible exploded, killing all aboard.

Others fell out of airborne craft and lived to tell about it. Johnny Mack, a well-known balloonist, made a number of flights from Million Dollar Pier. One day, though, a shift in the winds sent Mack twisting into city power lines instead of out to sea. City hall promptly banned all balloon ascensions from Absecon Island.

But there was no law against jumping into the ocean from blimps and helicopters. Joseph Hackney, Atlantic City fire chief and a performer in the diving show at Steel Pier in the forties, managed both: a 145-foot blimp drop, and a slightly shorter fall from a copter. (And speaking of helicopters: one flew Miss America around the *inside* of cavernous Convention Hall on December 1, 1973.)

There were stunts that bestrode the beach like colossi. For twenty-two years a typewriter 1,728 times normal size was on exhibit at the Garden Pier and later at Convention Hall. The Underwood Corporation had it built for the 1915 Panama-Pacific Exposition in San Francisco, then moved it to Atlantic City the next year. The typewriter's cost: $100,000. Each type bar weighed forty-five pounds, the carriage, thirty-five hundred, and it was over fourteen tons in all. The machine typed on stationery measuring nine by twelve feet; its ribbon was one hundred feet long and five inches wide. The typewriter's bell could be heard for blocks.

Visitors dictated messages to the machine's typist, or they sat down at the keyboard themselves. Vacationing secretaries had the most fun, frequently tapping out barbs to the boss back home:

```
My tYpust is on her vacation.
My trpists's awau fpr a week.
My trpudt us in her vacarion.
```

Life and times of a white elephant: Lucy was built in 1881 and used to lure real estate buyers to the shore. Then, for almost a century, she was left to crumble (opposite page).

In 1939 the Underwood giant typewriter was shipped to the New York World's Fair. It never returned to Atlantic City. With the outbreak of World War II, the amazing machine was dismantled, its metal parts donated to the scrap heap as a patriotic gesture.

Lucy the Elephant *always* seemed to have one foot in the scrap heap, ever to manage last-minute reprieves. James V. Lafferty started construction of the pachyderm in 1881, the first of a series of mammoth, animal-shaped structures he hoped to erect along America's eastern coast as land-sales promotions. Made of timber and sheet metal, Lucy stood sixty-five feet from toe to howdah. Her body was thirty-eight feet long and eighty-five feet around. Her trunk was thirty-six feet and flanked by two twenty-two-foot tusks. Lucy weighed ninety tons.

The elephant stands several miles south of Atlantic City, in Margate, where she was supposed to lure potential land buyers vacationing uptown. "South Atlantic City…sale of lots," read one of Lafferty's advertisements. "Elephant hotel affords grand view of surrounding country for miles around." Crowds flocked to the behemoth, climbing the spiral staircases in her hind legs, peering out the windows on

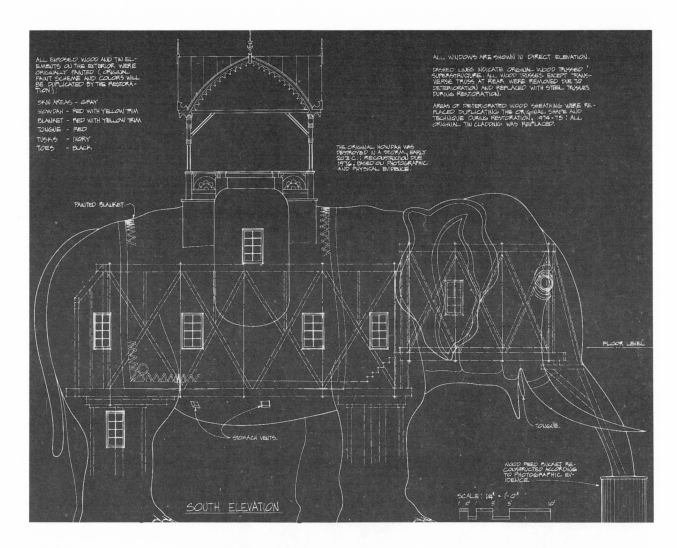

ALL EXPOSED WOOD AND TIN EL-
EMENTS ON THE EXTERIOR WERE
ORIGINALLY PAINTED (ORIGINAL
PAINT SCHEME AND COLORS WILL
BE DUPLICATED BY THE RESTORA-
TION):

SKIN AREAS - GRAY
HOWDAH - RED WITH YELLOW TRIM
BLANKET - RED WITH YELLOW TRIM
TONGUE - RED
TUSKS - IVORY
TOES - BLACK

ALL WINDOWS ARE SHOWN IN DIRECT ELEVATION.

DASHED LINES INDICATE ORIGINAL WOOD TRUSSED
SUPERSTRUCTURE. ALL WOOD TRUSSES EXCEPT TRANS-
VERSE TRUSS AT REAR WERE REMOVED DUE TO
DETERIORATION AND REPLACED WITH STEEL TRUSSES
DURING RESTORATION.

AREAS OF DETERIORATED WOOD SHEATHING WERE RE-
PLACED DUPLICATING THE ORIGINAL SHAPE AND
TECHNIQUE DURING RESTORATION, 1974-75 ; ALL
ORIGINAL TIN CLADDING WAS REPLACED.

THE ORIGINAL HOWDAH WAS
DESTROYED IN A STORM, EARLY
20TH C.; RECONSTRUCTION DUE
1976, BASED ON PHOTOGRAPHIC
AND PHYSICAL EVIDENCE.

PAINTED BLANKET.

FLOOR LEVEL

TONGUE.

STOMACH VENTS.

WOOD FEED BUCKET RE-
CONSTRUCTED ACCORDING
TO PHOTOGRAPHIC EV-
IDENCE.

SCALE: 1/4" = 1'-0"

SOUTH ELEVATION

In the summer of 1970, Lucy the eyesore was moved, reconstructed, and painted to be preserved forever as a museum. Above, *an architect's drawing of Lucy, 1976.*

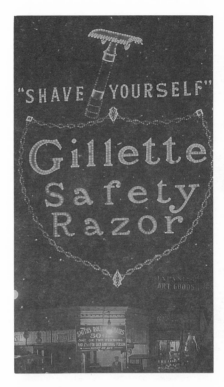

Boardwalk electric signs, circa 1910.

both sides of her body, trudging on up to the howdah, where they considered the sand-cheap, undeveloped real estate.

In 1887, Lucy was used simply as a tourist trap, then a tavern, finally as a summer cottage available for rent. For much of her subsequent life, however, she lay empty, her chipping paint and decaying skin giving her all the earmarks of a classic white elephant. Concerned citizens were forever raising funds to save her from total extinction. Relief came once and for all in 1966 when Lucy was designated a state, and later a national, landmark. Today, she a museum.

There were stunts that lit up the sky. Electricity was introduced to Atlantic City in 1882, marking the beginning of years of bright nights. In 1908, enormous electric signs sparkled on the Boardwalk, including a Gillette razor extravaganza housing fifteen hundred light bulbs, designed by Atlantic City's master sign-craftsman, Charles R. Lewin. Keen Kutter tools, Egyptienne Straights cigarettes, and Wrigley's Spearmint pepsin gum were but a few of the other awesome light shows. In 1954, electric light was one of the celebrated aspects of the city's Golden Days of Centennial. The occasion was marked by the switching on of the world's largest lightbulb: a seventy-five thousand-watt beacon donated by General Electric.

There were stunts that made you proud to be a servant. Each year Atlantic City's hotels, motels, and restaurants would hold their skills competition, in which workers square off in such national pastimes as turkey carving, bed making for maids, the waiters' hand-tray race, and the bellmen's relay. The capper was the selection and coronation of Atlantic City's prettiest waitress (one of the entrants was Ali MacGraw).

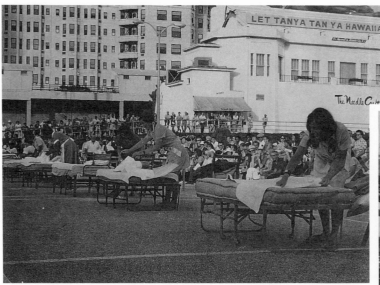

Scenes (from the 1950s) of the annual Hotel-Motel-Restaurant Skills Contest, in which waiters, busboys, bellhops, chambermaids, and chefs competed in a variety of events.

The contests are for professionals only, grueling tests of domestic proficiency. For example, judging rules for the turkey-carving championship note that fifty points are to be awarded for "consistency of portions," thirty-five for "cleanliness of carcass," ten for "ease of carving," and five for "overall neatness." The weight of the official tournament turkey is twenty-five pounds. Time limit: ten minutes.

There were stunts carved of sand. The city ordinance that kept business away from the ocean side of the Boardwalk didn't prevent creative types from setting up shop and making a few dimes. The earliest known sand artist was Philip McCord who, in 1897, sketched and sculpted a variety of scenes on the beach. Strollers were none too subtly advised that their donations were welcome. Other artists, their keen eyes flashing, following McCord's lead and arrived with their own shovels.

Over the years the open-air studios gave the public what it wanted. Woodrow Wilson was a popular subject of his day, as were caricatures of the kaiser and Charles Lindbergh. During slow news periods, the artists fell back on reproductions of famous paintings, such as *Washington Crossing the Delaware*. Religious and civic themes were abundant : a life-size crucifixion, for instance, or King Neptune seated on a seashell throne, emblematic of the spirit of Atlantic City.

And who knows what other masterpieces were created, only to be leveled by stormy weather? The sand artists, a versatile lot, took to adding one part cement to every three parts sand, thus gaining some protection against the elements. Still, a stiff blast like the '44 hurricane would come along to lay waste to the joys forever. And that's exactly what happened: when the winds died down and the dust settled, critics of sand art officially banned the studios from the beach.

There were stunts that gurgled "I do." In 1944, Ruth Ehlers, nineteen, married Louis Villani, twenty-three, both of North Bergen, New Jersey, in a diving bell thirty feet beneath Steel Pier. Included in the ceremony was seven-year-old Vicki Gold, flower girl, the chief compiler of the book you are reading.

In 1976, Mr. and Mrs. William Cravens were married in scuba gear, as performing mammals frolicked around, in the dolphin tank at Steel Pier. The ceremony, performed by Atlantic City's mayor, was witnessed by three hundred people.

There were stunts that masqueraded as human weirdos. The city was going through one of its periodic honor-the-Sabbath wars when, in 1901, Mayor William Stoy fingered the Wild Man of Borneo as the sort of nonessential "desecration" the resort could live without. Manacled and dressed in animal skins, the Wild Man spent his days in a caged pit under the Boardwalk, chewing on a raw bone, scaring the bloomers off passersby. Children shrieked; grown men and women recoiled at his fury. But everyone just gaped as Constable George Herbert, waving a warrant

Sand artists demonstrated their craft on the beach from 1897 through 1944. Boardwalk passersby threw coins to the artists, who in the 1930s earned more than fifty dollars a week.

FLYING FUR: In the thirties, animal acts went over big at Steel Pier. Professor Nelson's Boxing Cats slugged it out daily (above); *Captain Roman Proske danced with a tiger to the strains of Abe Lyman and His Californians* (opposite page, top); *Primo Carnero boxed a kangaroo* (opposite page, inset).

issued by Mayor Stoy, entered the pit to arrest the Wild Man for performing on Sunday. Spectators were convinced that Constable Herbert was but a step away from becoming so many raw bones. But the Wild Man of Borneo, later identified as "Brownie" the rolling-chair pusher, meekly complied and followed Herbert into his paddy carriage.

Finally, there was the High Diving Horse. This was the stunt featured on so many billboards, postcards, magazines, and vacation snapshots that it emerged as the icon of the Queen of Resorts. For twenty-five years, until she "got a little heavy in 1930," Lorena Carver plunged on horseback from a forty-foot tower into a pool on Steel Pier. Lorena was the daughter of Dr. W. F. Carver, a Wild West showman who thought a pretty girl would liven up his flagging diving horse act. Up went Lorena, then down, then up, then down, averaging a broken bone a year, creating a carnival legend.

It wasn't as hard as it looked—for the horse or the rider. "All the girl has to do is look pretty and not fear height or water," Lorena said after she'd retired to train later generations of jumpers. "The horse knows what to do. He'll take care of you." As for the horses, she continued, they loved it. The biggest problem was getting them to delay their leaps in order to build suspense.

Quarter horses were used for the stunt, most of them living to the grand old age of forty or more. Some stood on the platform for as long as five minutes, gazing at sea gulls or the crowd below, others reached the precipice and plopped right in. "The horse who does the most graceful dive just gets up on the tower and jumps," Lorena explained. "You can lead a horse to water, but you can't teach him showmanship."

Over the years dozens of riders performed the act, including Jaque Leeman, Elsa Rohr, Arnette Webster, Sonora Carver (who was blind), Olive Gelnaw, and

THE THRILL OF A MINUTE.
THE FAMOUS FORTY FOOT PLUNGE ON HORSEBACK —
ATLANTIC CITY STEEL PIER

The High Diving Horse was for decades the best-known stunt of all. These are but a few of the ladies and mounts who took the forty-foot plunge: Lorena Carver on John the Baptist (with Sonora Carver holding the reins), circa 1929.

Right, *Sonora on Red Lips, circa 1933; left, the "Low Diving Jackasses" from the Steel Pier Water Circus took turns with the High Diving Horse in 1945; Marion Hackney (below), emerging on Dimah (Steel Pier owner Hamid spelled backwards), circa 1954.*

Marion Hackney, the daughter of the man who jumped out of helicopters and blimps. Miss Hackney debuted in 1953, closing her eyes, hanging on for dear life. The first time was the hardest. "It's fun," she told a reporter soon thereafter. "You never know how the horse is going to hit the water. The other day he went sideways. It knocked the wind right out of me."

The *New York Times* remarked in 1929: "Atlantic City is the apotheosis of publicity. It is the crescendo of horn-tooting." Indeed, it was America's brassiest band of the century, playing summertime loony tunes on land, at sea, from the air. The music carried far and wide, luring visitors by the millions. And by the time they'd packed and left Atlantic City, nearly every one of them was ready for a rest.

In 1940 midget bellhops (opposite page) *led a rolling-chair procession complete with brass band. Above, Lyndon Johnson immortalized in wax, 1964.*

Easter in Atlantic City, 1940.

INTERMISSION:
GREETINGS FROM
ATLANTIC CITY

Between the Boardwalk and the sea there is at low tide a great strip of sand which is probably white at the beginning of summer, but which assumes the colour of pepper and salt after a few millions of human animals have wallowed in it during the heated season.

From an article in the *Bookman*,
XXX, September, 1909

A VACATIONER, YOU CHECKED IN with the weight of the world on your shoulders, and checked out with a suntan. A honeymooner, you arrived with your chastity, and left with a glow. A conventioneer, you filled out your name tag, and proceeded to let off some steam.

Whatever you were, when you set out for Atlantic City, you left the Protestant ethic on your doorstep. the *New York Times* observed in the late twenties that "in New York, play is unfortunately adulterated with work. But in Atlantic City, work is not even a grim spectre in the background."

Indeed, the city was called "The World's Playground," and it was hard to resist. On the morning of your first day, you kept a straight face, determinedly. Then, after a short while in the sun and air (is ozone the oxygen of the devil?), your common sense took a vacation of its own. You lay out on the beach too long. Your first stroll down the boards gave you blisters. By nightfall, your very soul was aflame—and you thought you came down here to relax!

In this playground, single women were especially vulnerable to serpents in the sandbox. "Thus it is," wrote a reporter in 1906, "that women who in their home towns are wholly decorous and will never go to anything more exciting than an ice-cream sociable, or the strawberry festival of the First Presbyterian Church will, in Atlantic City, be absolutely careless about the minor *mores*. One of these women, staying alone at a hotel, will, after the third meal, become acquainted with some man who sits at the same table with her. On the next day she will be rolling with him in a 'chair,' while in less than a week she will be visiting 'grottoes' with him in the evening, and drinking 'highballs.'"

Atlantic City made fools of us all. A newspaper account (1928) described "the wheel chairs [going by] in steady procession, from early morning till late at night: a man with two girls; a woman in bright purple, wearing eye-glasses, trying to look bored and not quite succeeding; an unshaven gentleman alone—he has one foot over the dashboard so that all the world can view his brown socks with the white clockings; three girls, with challenging eyes for amateur sheiks; a fat red gentleman smoking a fat black cigar, and trying to look as though he had spent all his life traveling in rolling chairs."

Yes, some of us went to see and be seen.

In the prepolyester age, the Boardwalk was witness to the latest fashions. A

The first annual Board-walk Easter Parade was held in 1876. Above, an Easter Sunday mob scene, circa 1915.

1926 interview with Samuel P. Leeds, director of the Chamber of Commerce, related that "no matter whether they come from a big city or a little town, no matter whether they stop at some modest house…or in one of the biggest, most luxurious ocean-side hotels, the women who come here have obviously new frocks, hats, and shoes, bought to be shown off on the Boardwalk."

And alongside them there were more than a few peacocks among the Boardwalk pigeons: "If the men who accompany [these women] claim not to like it," Leeds continued, "well, they are dressed up considerably themselves."

Sartorial splash was never more eye catching than at the Easter Parade. The first was in 1876, when a great spillover from the Philadelphia Centennial Exposition was expected but not realized. The parade took place under overcast skies, and there was little to suggest the vitality of future happenings (save for Isaac Forrester's ever-spinning Epicycloidal Diversion and other Boardwalk oddities).

By century's end, though, Atlantic City's Easter Parade was an explosion of

Atlantic City has drawn millions of out-of-towners in their spring finest. Shown here are fashions from 1923.

imported fabrics and lace. In 1902, said the local paper, the most popular bonnets were "mostly broad-brimmed, trimmed with large roses and almost covered with chiffon and violets." Three years later, the "waving plumes and lace...suggest an exaggerated flower bed."

By the twenties, a visit to the Easter Parade was the fashion plate's notion of a holy pilgrimage. The observant Samuel Leeds recalled: "One Easter was raw and chill. It was about the time sleeveless dresses came in for daytime wear, and the most sensible of the paraders hid their new frocks under fur coats. But not the young girls. Chill winds or not, these dresses had to show, and hundreds of bare arms paraded the Boardwalk, red arms, goose-fleshed arms, arms blue with cold, but the girls who owned them were impervious to discomfort. What if they did sneeze for a week after, they were showing off a new fashion!"

Some of us went to play on the beach.

While a few diehards trickled into town during the winter, March and April were often the cruelest months for many who couldn't wait for Atlantic City's

Dolores Friedman, Easter Sunday, 1944.

Bonnet madness, 1961.

summer. But the end of May brought the warming sun; now the beaches came alive, and the fashions down there were something! City fathers, the ones who blithely looked past illegal gambling, all manner of vice, and Sunday liquor sales, kept a vigilant eye on public bathing morals, enforcing the city's tough bathing-suit code. In the years following the completion of the railroad, most male and female bathers played by the rules, he wearing long bathing trousers and a top, she in a flannel frock over ankle-length stockings. Each wore a straw hat and canvas shoes, at times into the water.

Of course there was always the bad apple. A postcard sent by a vacationer in 1897 told of a "young fellow who was dressed in a women's bath suit. It was white, with black braid trimmings, black stockings with white slippers, and black braid wound around the limbs, a la Roman style. The Kodak fiends were kept busy taking snap shots."

Back then the women left nothing to chance—or to nature. A city official at the turn of the century reported that "skirts were made with four buttons...in the back. That was so they could lose a button, even two, and still be safe."At

Easter on Arctic Avenue, 1952. Madame Sarah Spencer Washington (inset), who'd make a fortune manufacturing hair products, organized the Easter Parade for black residents in 1946.

AFTERNOONS ON CHICKEN BONE BEACH

The Atlantic City beach was, in fact, many beaches, with sections informally reserved for teenagers, old folks, and a variety of ethnic groups. The principal black beach was at the foot of Missouri Avenue. It is best remembered from the forties and fifties. Chris Columbo, a well-known black drummer at the Club Harlem, and Russell Le Van, a beach concessionaire, had these impressions.

COLUMBO: We used to go bathing at Indiana Avenue, till they finally built the Claridge Hotel. Then they would tell the people who worked in the hotels, "Don't go to Indiana Avenue any longer, because you make too much noise and disturb the guests…So instead we went to Missouri Avenue….

We named the area Chicken Bone Beach. Blacks, you see, knew how to fry chicken. Colonel Sanders still don't know how to cook chicken. It's all right long as it's *hot*, but blacks knew how to cook chicken that you could put in a little cake box, those round, tin cake boxes. You wrapped it in a towel…and ate it for four days, without it being refrigerated. It was always good….

And I can see why they called it Chicken Bone Beach—the people came down for a day and picnicked. And I wish to this day we had a beach,…where you could take your family and prepare some food.

LEVAN: All the excursions, your bus groups, used to come down, and they'd empty the bus right on the Boardwalk. And they'd all bring their sandwiches and chicken. We put up cabanas and we gave first-class equipment. We finally wound up getting the better trade, because in those days the black entertainers and the people liked to be together….

There was many a day when we'd have Sammy Davis, Jr., and the Mills Brothers, and Louis Jordan, and maybe Sugar Ray Robinson and Moms Mabley. And the showgirls from [Club] Harlem…. They called it Sunshine Row. They liked to sunbathe, believe it or not. That section I had to keep just for them…. They would put on all kinds of skits and all kinds of crazy stuff there, and I remember Sammy Davis used to hand one of the help his watch to keep. On the back was inscribed To THE GREATEST LITTLE ENTERTAINER IN THE WORLD, SAMMY DAVIS. FROM SAMMY DAVIS.

Peggy Thomas, a singer, on Chicken Bone Beach in the fifties.

During the twenties the city employed officers to walk the sands, enforcing the resort's bathing-suit regulations. Even as late as 1940 there was a law on the books requiring men to wear tops while on the beach.

least their *secrets* were safe: many women wore padding sewn into their suits, to fill out breasts, arms, shoulders, even calves. In the early 1870s, Atlantic City bathhouses *rented* such outfits to women who desired them.

Bathing bloomers caught on in 1907, though most women continued to wear stockings underneath. The more daring rolled down their hosiery, while the *most* daring went all the way: they discarded leg coverings entirely. Such offense was regarded as a definite step toward moral decay, prompting Beach Superintendent John T. Beckwith to spring into action. On August 25, 1907, Beckwith ruled that no lady would be allowed on the beach without stockings—and offenders would be punished to the full extent of the law.

In the twenties, Atlantic City deployed censors—with tape measures and arrest warrants—to cruise the beach in search of stockingless bathers. One censor was Edward Shaw, who had the misfortune of running into Louise Rosine, a thirty-nine-year-old novelist from Los Angeles. Officer Shaw stopped Miss Rosine at Virginia Avenue and the Boardwalk and informed her that those stockings rolled down below her knees were against regulations. Trying to be fair, Officer Shaw gave her the chance to roll them up. "I most certainly will *not*

Atlantic City's first full-time lifeguards, Dan Headley and Nick Jefferies, 1892.

roll them up," she retorted. "The city has no right to tell me how I shall wear my stockings," she said, according to the *New York Times*. "It is none of their darn business. I will go to jail first."

And go directly to jail she did, but not before she'd hauled off and smacked Shaw in the face, breaking his glasses. Rosine was booked for assault as well as on the stockings rap, issuing a statement from her cell that asserted her constitutional right to "bare feminine knees." If necessary, she said, she would fight the case to the Supreme Court. (History is silent about what happened next.)

At least the bathing suit laws weren't sexist—they treated *everyone* unfairly. Tops were strictly required for all males, and those without proper shirts were jailed regularly. It wasn't until 1940 that the city repealed the ordinance prohibiting men from going topless on the strand.

Some of us went to go swimming.

The beach at Atlantic City is one of America's best, a wide, gentle slope of fine-grained sand, slipping under the sea to provide relatively calm bathing conditions. Nevertheless, the city was diligent in its pursuit of safety.

Bathing at Atlantic City, N. J.

Floating at Atlantic City

In 1855, the resort hired its first "constable of the surf," William S. Cazier, who received $117 for a season's work. In 1870, a British tinkerer named Captain William Tell Street advanced the art of lifesaving with his patented "life lines for surf bathing." These were heavy cables—which bathers held onto—running from pilings on the beach to anchors offshore. Hotel brochures promoted them heavily; a reassuring poem was even written:

> *The Safety Lines*
> *Behold! Along the Atlantic Coast*
> *The cords upheld in air,*
> *See patriot flags by high winds tost:*
> *The safety lines are there,*
> *Beneath them rolls an angry foam,*
> *The bather in his glee,*
> *Feels in the water quite at home,*
> *From thought of danger free.*

A volunteer lifeguard force was established in 1872, the city-paid Beach Patrol not coming till twenty years later. Lifeguards sat in boats at varying intervals

MOMENTS TO REMEMBER...

*For over a hundred years, photo galleries
on the Boardwalk gave vacationers the chance to
preserve their memories of Atlantic City. Visitors posed on sets,
or behind painted flats, grinning at the camera—or trying to.
Some of the results are shown on the following pages in a portfolio of
souvenir photos. They proved we all hadn't dreamed this incredible place.
Atlantic City really existed, and we were there.*

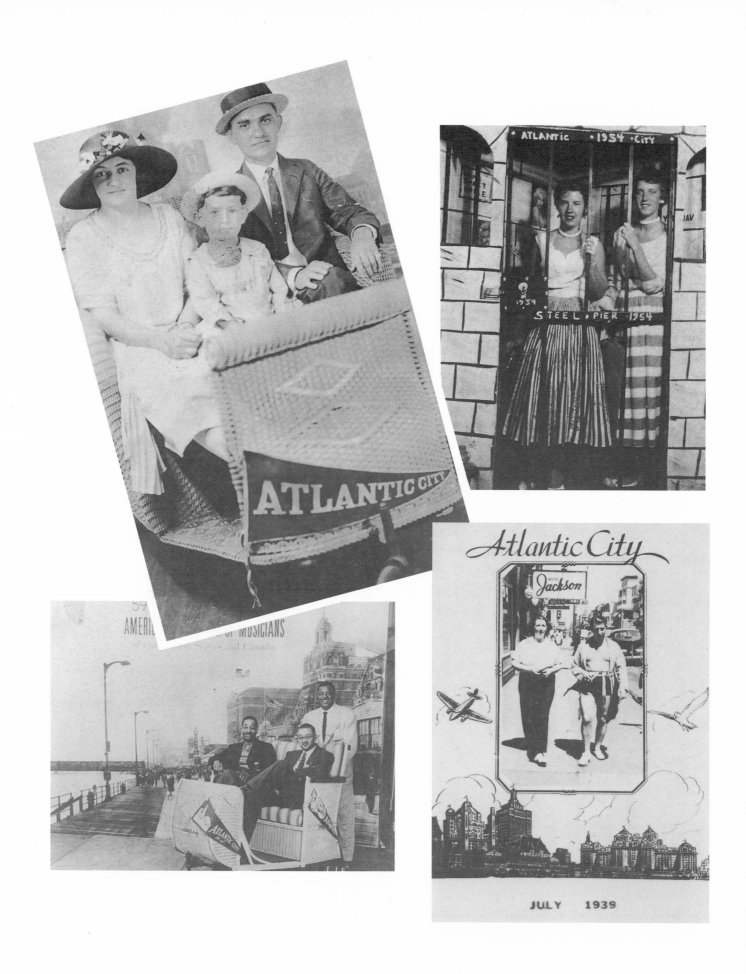

...AND HONEYMOONS TO REMEMBER.

During World War II, the resort hired—as a publicity stunt—a patrol of female surf watchers. Louise Lasser's mother, Ruth Goldberg, is extreme right.

offshore, surveiling the bathers and making sure no one swam beyond the flotilla. "This is a very wise move," agreed the *Philadelphia Inquirer*, "as fully 50 percent of the drowning cases of past seasons have resulted from persons getting out to sea so far that they had no strength left with which to return."

Atlantic City spokesmen always insisted that the cause of the accidents had nothing to do with tricky undertows but rather with human idiocy. Said one veteran of the Beach Patrol: "About all we ever drag out of the water are swimmers. Guys with muscles. A lot of them got an emblem on their trunks that says they're a senior lifesaver. They think they're in a big swimming pool. When something happens to them, they discover the ocean only has one side, not four."

During World War II, the Beach Patrol decided to turn a shortage of able-bodied lifeguards into a classic Atlantic City publicity stunt. It hired six beach belles to guard the bathers, including Ruth Goldberg, Louise Lasser's mother. Another was Grace Detig McGowan, who recalled: "It got to be too much for us because all the big he-men were getting into the water and yelling they were

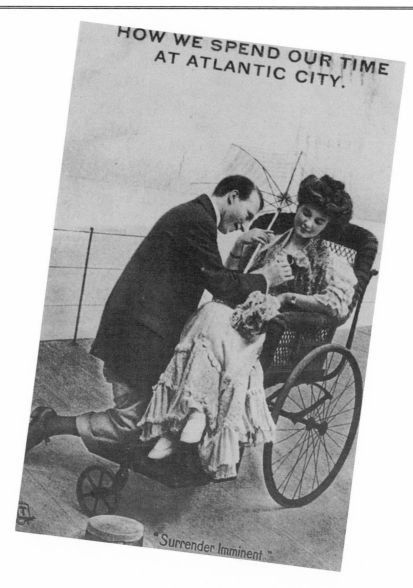

HOW WE SPEND OUR TIME AT ATLANTIC CITY.

"Surrender Imminent."

drowning just so the girls could rescue them." The lady lifeguards disappeared in short order, never to serve again until recent years, when fair-employment considerations enabled qualified women to join the A.C.B.P.

Some of us went to make love, to make deals, to make war.

Atlantic City's first recorded wedding and honeymoon took place on December 22, 1842, when Lovenia Adams married Joseph Showell. From that point on, the resort gained a reputation second only to Niagara Falls as the middle class's honeymoon haven.

And the city moved energetically to popularize its romantic image, releasing true love stories to the city newspapers. One example is from the *Philadelphia Inquirer*, 1893:

> A wedding will take place quietly at this resort tomorrow, which if all details were known, would disclose one of the most romantic stories of the season. The bride is a young Philadelphia girl who is well known among the employees of Wanamaker's, where she has held a position of saleswoman for several

years past. She came down last week to spend her vacation at the shore, and during the gay round of pleasure she encountered a young Western man [who is] reputed to be [from] one of the wealthiest families of Colorado.

You could spot the honeymooners a block away, as they window-shopped the Boardwalk, held hands along the ocean, or left the piers with giant pandas awarded at the games of skill or chance. Just as recognizable were the conventioneers, with their funny hats and midwestern twangs, not having the *vurry* good time Philadelphians had, but a *vairy* good time nonetheless.

The swarm was thickest around Convention Hall, officially Atlantic City Auditorium, seven acres of concrete located on the Boardwalk between Georgia and Mississippi. There's nothing very pretty about the hall, but as a collection of largests, bests, and firsts it stands as an appropriate monument to the American Ethos. When it opened on May 31, 1929, it was the largest building in the world without roof posts and pillars, and the hall's pipe organ was the biggest of its kind.

Unlike Lucy the Elephant, Convention Hall was prodigious with a purpose: to attract millions of dairy farmers, surgeons, ministers, architects, bankers, bakers, and all other convening working stiffs to Atlantic City. Conventioneers brought wives, kids, and pocket money, which kept the hotels, restaurants, piers, and theaters in the chips.

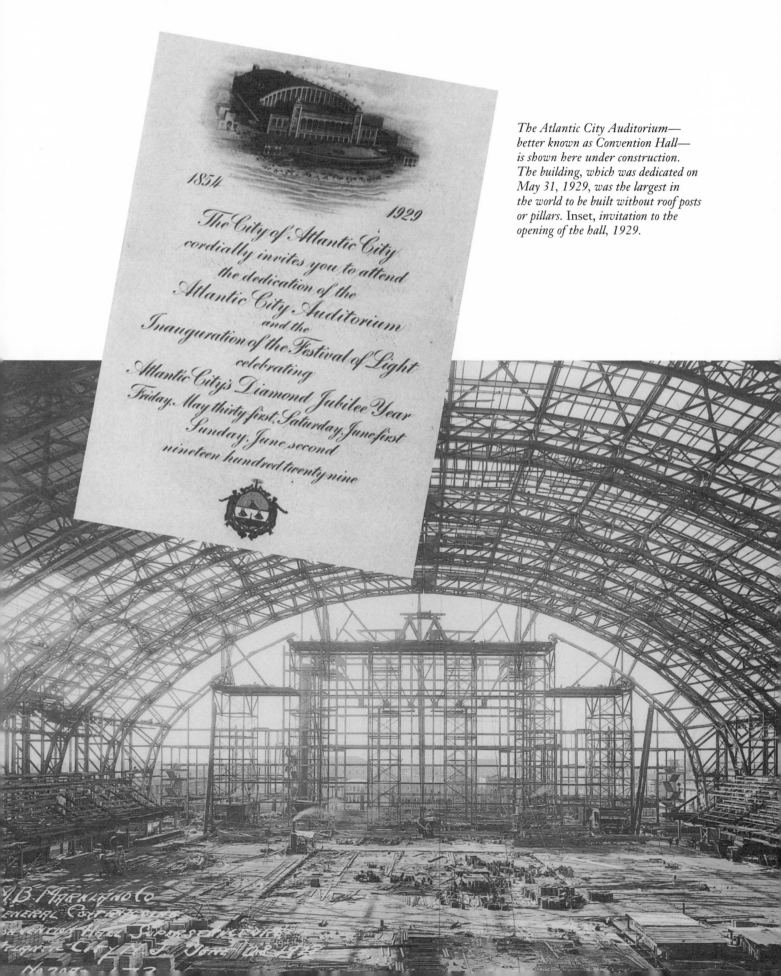

1854

1929

The City of Atlantic City
cordially invites you to attend
the dedication of the
Atlantic City Auditorium
and the
Inauguration of the Festival of Light
celebrating
Atlantic City's Diamond Jubilee Year
Friday, May thirty first, Saturday, June first
Sunday, June second
nineteen hundred twenty nine

*The Atlantic City Auditorium—
better known as Convention Hall—
is shown here under construction.
The building, which was dedicated on
May 31, 1929, was the largest in
the world to be built without roof posts
or pillars. Inset,* invitation to the
opening of the hall, 1929.

The Ice Capades (top) *visited Convention Hall every summer, beginning in 1941. The auditorium served as home ice to the* Atlantic City Sea Gulls (center), *a successful thirties semipro hockey team.* Convention Hall (bottom) *at night.*

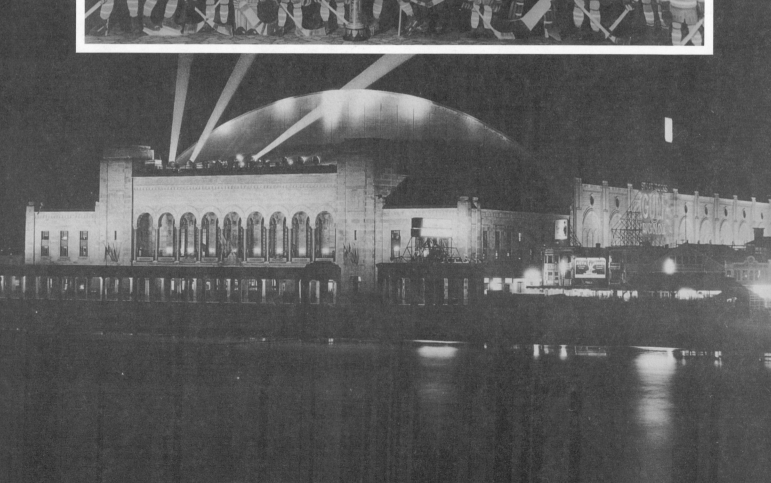

Convention Hall's pipe
organ (above) *was called
the largest in the world.
The instrument houses
32,913 pipes and 336
voices, including 22 percus-
sion instruments. In 1973
(inset)* a helicopter flew
Miss America around the
inside of the hall's main
floor.

105

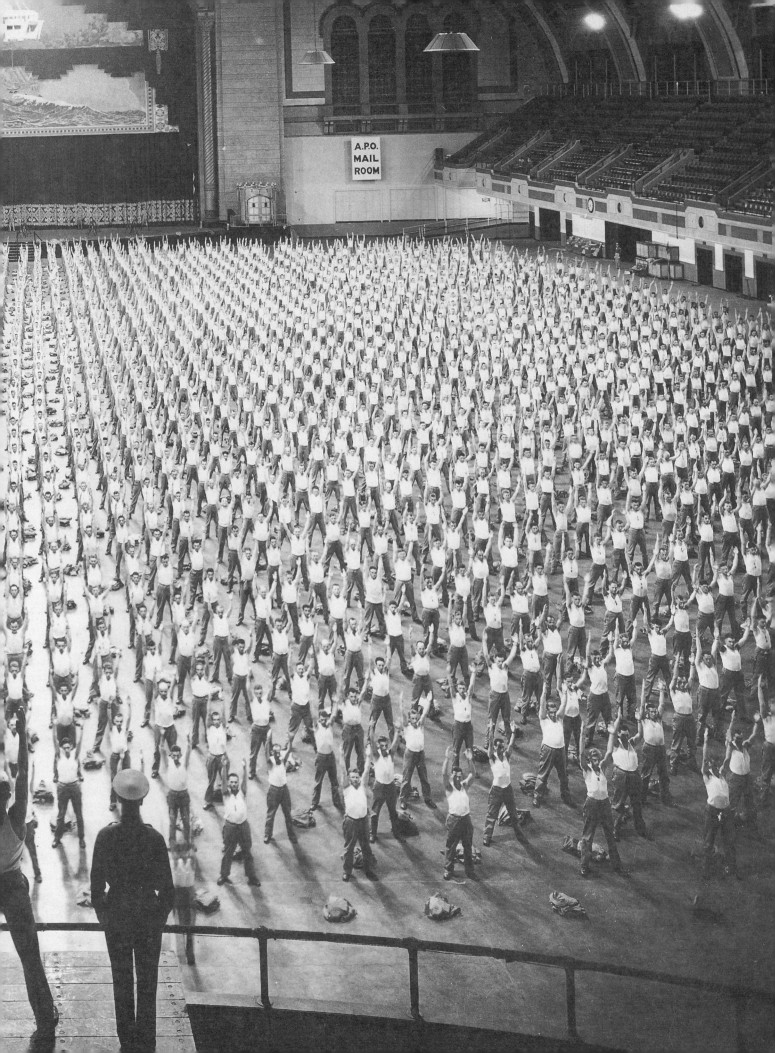

Top, *a decontamination squad on Boardwalk maneuvers, 1943. Inset, Milton Caniff's version of wartime Atlantic City, 1944. Right, members of Company B, 157th Field Artillery, training with machine guns atop the President Hotel, 1941.*

Top, *Easter Sunday, 1944.* Below, *a mock beachfront invasion, 1944.* Inset, *Marlene Dietrich at a war bond rally, 1942.*

Shriners' convention in the thirties.

Between these bookings, Convention Hall has served as the site of the Miss America Pageant, the annual summertime home of the Ice Capades, and was the scene of Lyndon Johnson's bittersweet 1964 nomination. The Atlantic City Sea Gulls, a tough semipro hockey team in the thirties, made its home rink in the hall, and the world's first indoor football game was played under the auditorium's roof.

NEVER DID THE HALL host a bigger event than during World War II, when the Army leased the arena as a training facility. Tens of thousands of Air Force personnel prepared for overseas service in Atlantic City. This was good for the country, doubly good for the resort, which faced a crippling loss of tourist revenue as a result of the war.

Calisthenics and briefings were conducted throughout the sprawling auditorium, while neighboring hotels were converted into barracks. By 1943, the Army had moved into such palaces as the Traymore, Breakers, Brighton, Shelburne, St. Charles, and Dennis, among others. For many GIs, basic training in Atlantic

City was the "life of Riley," even though the brass made a passing attempt to impose spartan conditions. "Lobbies, mezzanines, dining rooms, halls and other parts of the hotels were stripped of rugs, carpets, draperies, and other adornments," reported the *New York Times*. "Over the concrete of the floors march thousands of leather-heeled recruits. Most bedroom furniture has been replaced by army equipment."

To shopkeepers and restauranteurs, the occupation represented a blessing in uniform. Their gratitude was at times so great that the Army Air Force Basic Training Center issued warnings to the locals: "Civilians are requested not to overdo their hospitality toward soldiers in taverns. The result of buying drinks for a soldier is usually to get the soldier himself into trouble. The soldier who overindulges at night finds he cannot keep up with the rigorous training schedule of the following day. Such hospitality...actually operates to weaken our war effort."

In 1946 a delegation from the United Nations came to the resort to look it over as a possible permanent UN site.

The jitney (above) is a favored means of transportation in Atlantic City. The first jitneys rolled in 1915. Inset, Ben Hogan at the Atlantic City Country Club, 1954. The term birdie *was coined at the club in 1903.*

Rumors flew in the ocean breezes that German U-boats cruised along the coast. In March of 1942, a dimout was ordered for the city, and Boardwalk lamps were shaded on the ocean side. A malaria scare also occurred that year, though the outbreak was considerably less serious than Boardwalk chatter would have had you believe. On the lighter side, there was the documented adventure of the GI patrol that wandered into a nudist colony outside the city, its troops spending several pleasant hours playing volleyball and sunbathing with a group of naked women.

For thousands of airmen, the sojourn at the shore was their first taste of Atlantic City, and many would later return on their honeymoons and for business conventions. They thus joined the countless millions whose feet have walked the boards, tested the water, and whose children delighted in the sights and smells of this summertime playground.

Some of us went and never forgot it.

It was for the kids that Atlantic City reserved its warmest greetings. There was cotton candy, sizzling hot dogs, frozen custard, fresh peanuts and popcorn on nearly every corner. And, most of all, there was that moment when their heads touched down at night, when that ineffable aroma of the soft, damp pillow told them they were in Atlantic City—and no other place on earth.

AN ALBUM OF FAMILIES

Atlantic City is preserved in millions of snapshots: pictures pasted down with black paper corners, pictures in gold frames arranged on the dresser, pictures in plastic displayed on the desktop, pictures in billfolds, pictures on walls. These pages offer a sample of the pictures, culled from family albums that chronicle sweet life and good Atlantic City times of three generations of vacationers. It is in these snapshots that the real Atlantic City exists, the Atlantic City of our private memories.

The unmistakable Mr. Peanut, who greeted visitors outside the Planters Peanut store at Virginia and the Boardwalk.

Marilyn Monroe, grand marshal at the Miss America Pageant, 1952.

STARSHINE

THE HISTORY OF SHOW BUSINESS in Atlantic City is so rich, various, and central to American popular culture, it is difficult to know where, when, and how to raise the curtain. Taking a cue from the many others who have written about this circus, it is perhaps best to start with hyperbole, to offer some useful and curious believe-them-or-not facts:

If all the big bands that played Atlantic City played at once, their trombones would be heard as far away as Mars.

If the sheet music to songs written about, or in, Atlantic City were ever laid end to end, the line of paper would cover the Boardwalk.

If a theater-goer had attended consecutively every Broadway tryout in Atlantic City from 1901 to 1935, he would have spent nearly four months in his seat, twenty-four hours a day.

If it hadn't been for unique opportunities in Atlantic City, the American public might never have heard of John Philip Sousa, W. C. Fields, Paul Whiteman, and, for better or worse, Abbott and Costello.

And if Atlantic City ever decided to throw a party for itself, inviting a limited number of stars who shone brightly over the years, the guest list would include, for openers, Dean Martin, Jerry Lewis, Sophie Tucker, Billie Burke, Jimmy Durante, Helen Forrest, Red Skelton, Donald O'Connor, Milton Berle, Martha Raye, Ted Weems, Irving Berlin, Guy Lombardo, Bing Crosby, Bob Hope, Harry Richman, Frank Sinatra, Mack Gordon, Sammy Davis, Jr., Fred Waring, Ed Sullivan, Jackie Gleason, Perry Como, Rudy Vallée, Eleanor Powell, Mae Clarke, Joe E. Lewis, Tommy and Jimmy Dorsey, George Jessel, Benny Goodman, Harry James, Eddie Fisher, Joan Blondell, Eddie Cantor, Sammy Kaye, and Pinky Lee.

These were just a few of the names honored at the city's Centennial Celebration of 1954, a fraction of the names that have appeared in lights over the Boardwalk, or at clubs, on the piers, and in the hotels of Atlantic City. Missing are Flo Ziegfeld, George S. Kaufman, George Gershwin, George Abbott, Sarah Bernhardt, Fanny Brice, Victor Herbert, Enrico Caruso, Eubie Blake, Glenn Miller, and Harry Houdini, to list others who played leading parts in the development of Atlantic City entertainment.

What better place to take America's pulse?

What better place to find out what made the nation laugh, cry, or stomp its feet?

What better place to observe how Americans escaped their darkest moments, or reveled in their giddiest?

Below, *Alice Wagner Ettinger, a Ziegfeld girl, circa 1920.* At
right, *Margaret Price Cornell, a Ziegfeld 1928 girl born in
Atlantic City.* Bottom, *Frank Elliott's Steel Pier Minstrels, 1927.*
*Minstrel troupes were popular in the resort for decades. W. C. Fields
got his start in one, as did Abbott and Costello and Pinky Lee.*

IN THE BEGINNING there was vaudeville. Late in the 1800s it was a melange of trained animal routines, blackface minstrel revues, and inane domestic sketches. Imagine a presentation on the order of "The Colored Heaven": showing a Southern colored man in one of his happiest moments. "'The Watermellon [*sic*] Song'… sung by Manual Roman." Or a musical interlude such as "Sadie, the Princess of Tenement Row," mounted to appeal to the predominantly working-class audience that frequented the Atlantic City theaters of the time.

But as Charles E. Funnell describes it in *By the Beautiful Sea*, vaudeville soon took a turn for the better. Showmen on the piers posted marquees announcing "Highclass Vaudeville," "Patronized by the Elite," "Ladies and Children Can Attend Unaccompanied." By 1900 you no longer had to hide your eyes beneath a straw hat when entering a vaudeville emporium. Atlantic City had become a vital staging ground for an emerging, and respectable, variety entertainment form.

One of the period's leading draws was John Murphy and his Original Murphy's Minstrels, including "America's Greatest Comic Juggler," none other than W. C. Fields, who'd worked his way up from his first professional booking at Fortescue's beer garden.

Above, *George W. Rowland, a vaudeville juggler, circa 1908. Rowland, who was never without his teddy bear, played various amusement piers.* Left, *Harry Houdini drew gasps on Garden Pier, circa 1917.*

Evelyn Nesbit and son Russell Thaw in a Boardwalk rolling chair, 1923. Smith and Dale (left) performed their classic lawyer routine—shown here in 1928—at several Boardwalk vaudeville theaters.

It was there Fields performed his juggling routines, at ten dollars a week, taking time off to shill for the establishment. According to McMahon's *So Young…So Gay!*, the young entertainer would pretend to drown in the ocean, whereupon his rescuers carried him back into Fortescue's, a fearful crowd in tow. As Fields hovered 'twixt life and death, the worried onlookers gave drink orders to the waiters. Then, as Fields recovered, additional orders toasted his good fortune.

Later in his career, Fields told interviewers that the drowning stunt had turned him against water forever. Though he owned homes with swimming pools, he said, not once did he ever get wet. "I once drowned twelve times a day for two weeks," he explained. "Would *you* like to swim if you'd drowned one hundred and sixty-eight times?"

Famed revues featuring girls, girls, and more girls opened in the century's first decade and became perennial Boardwalk smashes. The first *Ziegfeld Follies* debuted

George Jessel married Norma Talmadge in Atlantic City on April 23, 1934. Mayor Harry Bachrach officiated. Inset, Barbara Stanwyck, then Ruby Stevens, was a show girl at the Café Beaux Arts, 1926.

at Atlantic City in 1906, moving to Broadway the following year. Produced by Flo Ziegfeld and his wife, Anna Held, the *Follies* had more beautiful chorines than you could shake a leg at. Patricia Ziegfeld, Flo's daughter, recalled in *The Ziegfeld's Girl* (1964): "They were individually costumed, they danced with spirit, they paid attention to what was going on, and, most amazingly, they smiled—really smiled, as though they were having a perfectly wonderful time."

Florenz Ziegfeld, for all his success in Atlantic City, was never particularly fond of the resort. In fact, he dreaded it. "It was usually too cold to go swimming when we were there," Patricia wrote, "and the sight of all those salt-water taffy stands seemed to have a depressing effect....

"The whole Boardwalk routine was a tremendous bore, except for a toothpaste-manufacturing exhibit which, for some reason, he found absolutely fascinating. He hated brushing his teeth, but he would stare glassy-eyed...watching the toothpaste ooze out of a vat in a silent, gliding ribbon and disappear into waiting

Ring Lardner (above), *at the helm, and friends at a Boardwalk photo gallery in the early twenties.* Below, *the cast of* The Little Show, *words by Howard Dietz, music by Arthur Schwartz, 1929. The stars were Clifton Webb (front left), Fred Allen (right), and Libby Holman (center).* Inset, *Al Jolson (center) stood guard in the twenties.*

tubes.... It was all I could do to drag him away from the display, and when I finally managed it he would look back longingly over his shoulder as long as the exhibit was in sight."

The other famous troupes settled in for summer-long stints at the Boardwalk theaters and piers: *George White's Scandals, Earl Carroll's Vanities, Andre Charlot's Revue,* and more. Rudy Vallée starred in White's show; Beatrice Lillie made her first stage appearance in Charlot's, teaming up with Gertrude Lawrence in sketches such as "Cigarette Land," in which the cast of characters included Egyptian, Turkish, Russian, Scented, French, Cigar, Snuff, Chewing Tobacco, and Smoke.

Anyone who was anyone played Atlantic City. Joe Smith, of Smith and Dale, first appeared at the resort in 1903, "when the crowds on the Boardwalk made it very slow walking." In 1934, vaudevillian George Jessel married actress Norma Talmadge, at a ceremony performed by Mayor Harry Bachrach in the apartment of political kingpin Nucky Johnson. Five years later, Jessel met a husky sixteen-year-old Atlantic City lifeguard. His name was Toots Shor.

Eddie Cantor, Al Jolson, Irving Berlin, Tallulah Bankhead, Ruby Keeler, Penny "Blondie" Singleton, Ethel Waters, Fanny Brice, George Raft, Barbara Stanwyck, Ann Miller, who *didn't* know the way to Atlantic City? Some stars were even raised there, including Ed Wynn, Imogene Coca, Helen Forrest, George DeWitt, trumpeter Ziggy Ellman, Eleanor Powell, Mae Clarke (best remembered for Cagney's grapefruit scene), Phyllis Newman, and top model Candy Jones.

Ed Wynn (left), *who was raised in Atlantic City, visited his mother on States Avenue. Eddie Cantor* (above) *visited the beach in the thirties.*

Dorothy Lamour (above left) *joined Ronald Reagan and Jane Wyman* (above right) *at the Variety Club Parade of Stars in 1941.*

The fabulous Warner Theatre, dedicated on June 19, 1929.

Why, this town was stage struck! In addition to vaudeville, legitimate theater found vast audiences at the shore, the resort serving as a major East Coast tryout site. Over the first three-and-a-half decades of the century, more than eleven hundred plays broke in at Atlantic City. As a laboratory for hopeful producers, the city was ideal: close enough to New York, with large, cosmopolitan audiences, its theaters well equipped to accommodate the most ambitious productions.

Oliver Hardy was marshal of the 1941 Variety Parade, leading a star-filled motor-cade down the Boardwalk.

There is some doubt as to which was the first play to try out before moving to the Great White Way. Constance Barrie Martin, an historian of the theater, cites *Her Majesty, the Girl Queen of Nordenmark*, 1900, as the most likely. (Other fetching titles that season included *The Rogers Brothers of Central Park* and *Captain Jinks of the Horse Marines*.) Better-known tryouts would follow: *What Every Woman Knows* (1908), by James M. Barrie; *Peg O'My Heart* (1912), produced by Oliver Morosco; *The Boomerang* (1915), produced by David Belasco; *The Gold Diggers* (1918), by Avery Hopwood; *Abie's Irish Rose* (1922), by Anne Nichols; *The Show-Off* (1923), by George Kelly; *The Student Prince* (1924), a Shubert production; and *The Constant Sinner* (1931), written by, and starring, Mae West. And not to be omitted is Thornton Wilder's *The Skin of Our Teeth* (1942), the second act of which takes place in Atlantic City. The playwright worked on the production during frequent visits to the shore.

In contrast to the carefree mood of most visitors to Atlantic City, the play-wright, director, or producer in town with a new play was often a jangle of nerves. Moss Hart, in *Act One*, spoke for many theater people when he recalled the days before the opening of *Once in a Lifetime*, coauthored with George S. Kaufman:

Atlantic City as cast in the movies: June Haver and George Montgomery (right) on the beach in Three Little Girls in Blue. *Released in 1946, this film featured the song "On the Boardwalk (in Atlantic City)," specially written for the movie. Brad Taylor, Constance Moore, and Jerry Colonna as Neptune (below) starred in* Atlantic City, *1944.*

"Atlantic City in the spring of 1930 was busting at the seams.... I stared down from my hotel window at the sparkling ocean and at the pleasant pattern the strollers made along the sun-splashed boardwalk, and alert as always for omens, good or bad, I told myself that these holiday-minded folk were bound to be a good audience for a new comedy. Though I could not see their faces clearly, I preferred to imagine them as already wreathed in smiles of good will. After all, I thought reassuringly, Atlantic City was the top tryout town on the Eastern Seaboard, and the audience that would file into the Apollo Theatre on Tuesday night would not only be a knowledgeable one, but an understanding and forgiving one as well, for they were used to tryouts here and did not expect a new play to be airtight. They would accept its lacks as part of the whole holiday spirit that pervaded the resort itself." (In fact, the play was a hit.)

Jack Nicholson and Bruce Dern (above left) *starred in* The King of Marvin Gardens, *1972. Jayne Mansfield in* The Burglar, *1957, which was set in Atlantic City.*

George Abbott summed up his experiences more succinctly: "Atlantic City is a wonderful place to try out; you can go swimming."

And Ring Lardner, who came to down with *June Moon*—only to find that the play started out well, then sagged—was strolling disconsolately on the boards when he ran into a friend. "What are you doing in Atlantic City?" the friend wondered. Said Lardner without a pause: "I'm here with an act."

They were *all* there with acts—with hits, with flops, with hopes, with crashing disappointments:

1919: Alfred Lunt and Helen Hayes in *Clarence*. Ethel Barrymore in *Déclassé*.

ATLANTIC CITY BANDSTAND: at right, Harry James and Frank Sinatra (front row center), 1939. Below, *Vincent Lopez and His Latin Rhythms cooling off, 1939.*

The Glenn Miller Orchestra (top), *1938; Rudy Vallée and His Connecticut Yankees* (center), *1933; the Isham Jones Orchestra* (bottom), *1932.*

Clockwise, from top left: Count Basie and songwriter Benny Davis ("Margie") with radio host Barry Gray, a native son, 1947; Irving Berlin fishing in the thirties; Paul Whiteman and admirers, 1953; Sammy Kaye, swinging and swaying with Miss Atlantic City, 1949.

1921: George M. Cohan in *The Tavern*. Eva Le Gallienne in *Liliom*. Eddie Cantor in *Make It Snappy*.

1922: The Marx Brothers in *I'll Say She Is!* Billie Burke in *Annie Dear*. Jeanne Eagels in *Rain*.

1925: Al Jolson in *Big Boy*. Adele Astaire in *Lady Be Good*.

1926: George Arliss in *Old English*. Fred Astaire in *Funny Face*. Fanny Brice in *Fanny*.

1927: Irene Dunne in *Luckee Girl*. Claudette Colbert in *The Gringo*. Humphrey Bogart in *Saturday's Children*. Bill Robinson in *Brown Buddies*.

1929: Mae West in *Diamond Lil*. Spencer Tracy in *Salt Water*.

THOSE WHO DIDN'T MAKE IT in person made it to Atlantic City on film. The resort and the movies go back a long way. Thomas Edison, inventor of the movie camera, loved to go fishing with Million Dollar Pier's John Young and experimented with his device on the Boardwalk and beach. But even before, penny arcades along the walk offered crude moving picture machines consisting of revolving cards viewed through a peephole.

The first movie house was the Bijou on Atlantic Avenue, which opened in 1903. Like movie theaters elsewhere, the early Atlantic City houses were converted storefronts, reserved a few nights a week for the showing of this novelty called flickers.

By the twenties, palatial movie theaters graced the shoreline, assuming their proud places among the hotels. The most striking was the Warner, dedicated by Harry M. Warner on June 19, 1929. "Even if we lose money on it," Warner told a Boardwalk audience, "the project will represent a sound investment in as much as people from the world over will visit the place."

And what a place! Behind the terra-cotta facade, past the copper and plate-glass marquee, through bronze doors was a tiled lobby lined by six gold-framed mirrors. The foyer had terrazzo floors, marble wainscoting, and valuable oil paintings. Inside the auditorium the ceiling was painted to resemble a blue sky, in which small, twinkling lights were embedded. More than forty-two hundred plush seats faced an eighty three-foot-high stage. All this and air-conditioned too.

Warner needn't have been concerned about the future of movies in Atlantic City—especially in 1929. With the coming of the Depression, legitimate theater—with its relatively high ticket prices and steep production costs—faded at the resort. So everyone went to the movies. The big names in town, the live performers and stage actors, were replaced by the movie stars who dropped in for world premieres and general promotion: Tom Mix, Bob Hope, Jane Russell, Betty Grable, Roy Rogers, George Raft, Esther Williams, and others.

Atlantic City went movie crazy. As far back as 1922, the Miss America Pageant offered studio screen tests as part of its prize package. The tradition carried into the thirties; a newspaper account reported that one of the aims of the pageant was to "choose a girl who would 'click' in the movies.... In that way, the spectacle may be built into a national institution." And, in fact, a few familiar faces were uncovered, as we will see.

Burt Bacharach, age two-and-a-half, at his home by the shore, 1931.

Miss Atlantic City and well-known model Candy Jones, 1941.

The city itself made guest appearances in the movies: *Citizen Kane, Atlantic City* (a 1944 release with cameos by Paul Whiteman and Louis Armstrong), *The Burglar* (with Jayne Mansfield), *Funny Lady, The King of Marvin Gardens*, and *Three Little Girls in Blue*, released in 1946 and starring June Haver, Vivian Blaine, Vera-Ellen, George Montgomery, Frank Latimore, and Celeste Holm.

It was from this last that the resort inherited its best-known song, "On the Boardwalk (in Atlantic City)," music by Josef Myrow, lyrics by Mack Gordon. The song got its first exposure at the Miss America Pageant of 1946. Though the songwriters did not set out to compose "On the Boardwalk" as the town's municipal anthem, it became just that—in 1954 it was voted the official song of the Centennial.

The only other serious contender was the bouncy old-time favorite, "By the Beautiful Sea," written by Harry Carroll in 1914. Carroll, an Atlantic City native

Little Miss Atlantic City,
Phyllis Newman, 1939.

(b. 1892), went on to enjoy immense popularity as a songwriter. His credits include "Trail of the Lonesome Pine" and "I'm Always Chasing Rainbows."

From here competition doesn't merely slide downhill, it falls on its ear. Let's see …there was "Dear Remembrances of Atlantic City, N.J." (1896), by Reuben and Frank, part of which goes:

> *There pleasure grand on sea and land*
> *Whom wisdom blest seeks peace and rest*
> *For all young people, love will be,*
> *The star to guide! The hope to see.*

Then there was "Skate with Me, Kate (at the Million Dollar Pier)" (1903); "On the Old Front Porch" (1913), dedicated to Captain John L. Young; "Atlantic City All the Time" (1915), which was, for some strange reason, "approved by the Atlantic City Commissioners"; and "On the Pier" (1926), dedicated to Steel Pier owner Frank P. Gravatt.

Music written in Atlantic City about other themes was decidedly better. Irving Berlin spent many a summer trying out shows in Atlantic City. Some say he penned "A Pretty Girl Is Like a Melody" while sitting in a rolling chair; others insist that "All Alone" was written in similar circumstances. One thing is certain: Berlin's "Easter Parade" was written neither for, nor in, Atlantic City—though it is played there every year all the same.

The Black nightclub scene: the Sextuplets, performers at the Paradise, 1940 (above); Chorus girls at the Paradise, 1944.

Clockwise: the floor show at the Paradise, 1939. Ray Charles at Club Harlem in the 1960's . Christopher Columbus, who brought his Swing Crew to the Paradise and Harlem clubs in the forties and fifties.

The famed 500 Club, on South Missouri Avenue, was one of Atlantic City's prime show business centers. Included among the stars who sparkled there: Milton Berle and Sammy Davis, Jr., 1959 (above left); Dean Martin and Jerry Lewis with bandleader Peter Miller (above right), 1954; Sophie Tucker (center), 1952.

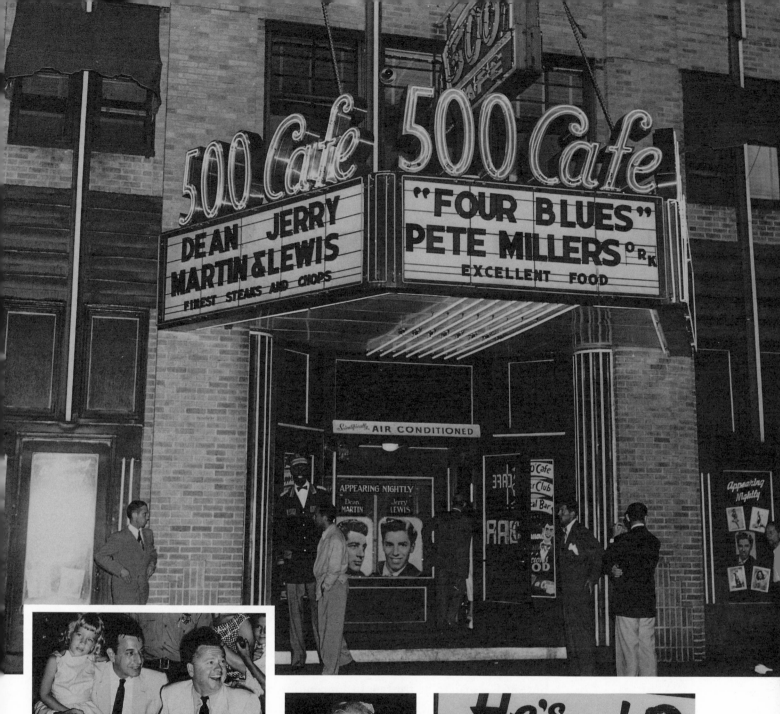

Opposite: *the sound of laughter, starring Horace McMahon (saxophone), Milton Berle (bass), Jackie Gleason (trumpet), and Frankie Hires (trombone), 1947.*

Stars were cemented in time at the entrance to the club. Far left, Mickey Rooney (with owner Skinny D'Amato and his daughter, Paulajane). Left, Jayne Mansfield getting plastered. Above, billboards heralding Frank Sinatra, 1960.

Joe DiMaggio and Jack E. Leonard in the fifties.

On questions of what was written where, reliable sources are hard to come by. Lou Cunningham, however, a longtime official at the Atlantic City Press Bureau, is a man to be trusted. In a recent interview, Cunningham noted the following, regarding the town as musical muse: Harry Tierney—best remembered for "Alice Blue Gown" (1919)—was a regular visitor to the shore, doing much of his writing there; George Gershwin, when starting out, plugged his songs on the Boardwalk; Benny Davis wrote "Margie" in front of the Ambassador Hotel; Gus Kahn, who wrote "I'll See You in My Dreams," collaborated for many years with bandleader Isham Jones, an Atlantic City fixture; Joe Burke, the Philadelphian who wrote "Tiptoe through the Tulips," spent much of his time at the resort; and finally there was Harry Links, "Mr. Tin Pan Alley," another boy from Philly, who composed "These Foolish Things" and "I'm Just Wild about Animal Crackers."

It really doesn't matter *where* the music came from—what matters is what it sounded like. And in Atlantic City it sounded sublime, from light opera performed on the piers to the big bands that thumped the ashtrays off the ballroom tables.

At the turn of the century, the city marched vigorously to the sound of brass,

John Philip Sousa keeping time. In 1903, George Tilyou of Steeplechase booked Sousa and his boys to play free concerts on the pier, later adding a popular vocal group to the bill, the Floradora Sextette. There was hardly a season for the next two decades that Sousa didn't set up shop in Atlantic City. This was partly due to the fact that in 1880 he'd married young Jennie Bellis, daughter of a Boardwalk photographer, who liked to return home every summer.

Atlantic City of the twenties and thirties offered the greatest big band music anywhere. At the hotels and piers, particularly Steel Pier, the immortal bands played to foot-stomping throngs.

Paul Whiteman, Bing Crosby, and the Rhythm Boys bounced the Grille at the Ambassador, where Whiteman advanced his reputation as the King of Jazz. He introduced "Whispering" at the resort, and it is said he recorded his two biggest hits there, "Avalon" and the Whiteman theme song, Gershwin's *Rhapsody in Blue*.

In the thirties, the Ambassador booked other ensembles, notably Isham Jones's band, which at one time included the young Woody Herman. Late in the decade, Harry James turned up for a July 4 date on Steel Pier with a skinny kid named

INKA DINKA DOO: Jimmy Durante on the Boardwalk in the fifties.

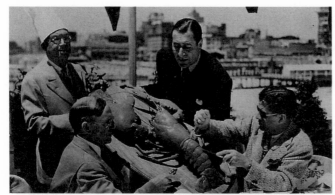

Top left: *Frank P. Gravatt (seated on the left) was Steel Pier's impresario from 1925 to 1945. The owner of Hackney's restaurant, Arthur Treacher (middle), and Rudy Vallée (right) gathered with Gravatt for a lobster feast, circa 1939. Center left, the Goldbergs on Steel Pier, 1934. Inset, Rex the Wonder Dog. The canine celebrity of Steel Pier's water show rode the waves with Arnette Webster, 1934. Below, Steel Pier at night, 1941.*

SOUSA (BUSTER KEATON AND DOUG FAIRBANKS) PAUSE A MOMENT BEFORE GENERAL MOTORS EXHIBIT. ATLANTIC CITY STEEL PIER

Sinatra; and in 1938, the pier hosted the first appearance of Gene Krupa's band, the one formed after he'd left the Benny Goodman organization. Then there were the swinging weeks and weekends of Count Basie, Duke Ellington, Stan Kenton, Buddy Rich, Les Elgart, Glenn Gray, Si Zentner, the Dorsey Brothers, and Glenn Miller, who recruited part of his renowned Air Force band from personnel stationed in Atlantic City. One such was an arranger Miller met at the shore, a soldier named Henry Mancini.

The vocalists were no less sweet sounding. "Baby" Rose Marie first played the Steel Pier when she was three, along with Rudy Vallée. Helen Forrest was another Atlantic City favorite, as were Vaughan Monroe, Kitty Kallen, Tony Bennett, Dinah Shore, Louis Prima, Ella Fitzgerald, Peggy Lee, and a roll call of others.

Across town, off the Boardwalk and down the side streets, the black night-clubs—particularly the Club Harlem—presented more sultry fare. Says Chris Columbo, a drummer at the Club Harlem and the famed Paradise Club: "The entertainment was 90 percent black. The trade was 90 percent white."

It was at the Paradise that a chorus girl named Carmen McRae was advised to take up singing; where the club's manager refused to hire Billy Eckstine at seventy five dollars a week, or Nat King Cole at two hundred dollars; where Peg Leg Bates, who wore different-colored artificial legs to match his tuxedos, danced and turned somersaults; where Count Basie bombed his first year, "because people [went] to the Paradise expecting to see a dozen beautiful chorus girls, half a dozen showgirls with…plumage in their hair, and a couple of acts, comics and dancers. They just weren't ready to sit down and listen to a concert," Columbo says.

Steel Pier, which opened in 1898, grew into Atlantic City's most celebrated entertainment spot. In 1927 John Philip Sousa sat in a rolling chair in front of the pier and was flanked by wax figures of Douglas Fairbanks and Buster Keaton.

The Three Stooges, typically serene, circa 1940.

Abbott and Costello (top), *who broke into Atlantic City as blackface comedians, wound up one of Steel Pier's most popular acts. In 1941 they visited the shore to promote their movie* Hold That Ghost. *Steel Pier was a showcase that attracted all the big names— and the big names who covered every move. Columnist Ed Sullivan* (left) *dropped by frequently in the late forties.*

In the fifties there was the renowned 500 Club, presided over by Paul "Skinny" D'Amato. Skinny could always count on an appearance by close friend Frank Sinatra, kept Sophie Tucker's name in lights, and helped launch the Will Mastin Trio with Sammy Davis. And it was D'Amato who first thought to combine the limp solo acts of a Jewish tummler named Lewis and an Italian crooner named Martin.

D'Amato recalls: "Jerry Lewis came in as a pantomime at $150 a week. Three weeks later Dean Martin came in as the singing act. Jerry went on first, then Dean. Jerry would run across the floor as Dean sang, throwing dishes. One night Dean grabbed Jerry by the neck and poured a pitcher of water over his pompadour. Jerry went into his monkey bit. It was the first time he ever did it, and it broke up the house. They started to do more together, dance, and kibbitz. They stayed all summer to packed houses."

Top, *Johnny Ray, without tears, Steel Pier, 1955.* Right, *Steel Pier favorites Frankie Avalon and Annette Funicello opened a Boardwalk bowling alley, once the site of the Warner Theatre, 1963.*

Where, you wonder, were the Ritz Brothers, Amos and Andy, Sally Rand, the Three Stooges, Ozzie Nelson, Gertrude Berg, Jackie Coogan, Kate Smith, Nelson Eddy, Jane Russell, Abbott and Costello, Bob Hope, Bunny Berigan, Red Norvo, Vincent Lopez, Phil Harris, Joe Penner, Edgar Bergen and Charlie McCarthy, Milton Berle, Burns and Allen, and Ben Blue?

And if Atlantic City was really the big deal we say, what about the Ink Spots, Gypsy Rose Lee, Helen Morgan, Jack Haley, Arthur Treacher, Martha Raye, Les Paul and Mary Ford, the Andrews Sisters, Red Buttons, the Four Aces, Paul Anka, Henny Youngman, Johnny Ray, Alan King, Dick Clark, and Dicky Do and the Don'ts?

They were all at the fabulous Steel Pier, where the music, the laughs, the movies, the theater, the dancing met the boxing cats, the performing chimps, the monster sea elephant, and—may he water-ski forever across Heaven's oceans—Rex, the Wonder Dog.

The Steel Pier was never modest about its virtues. Self-described as the "Showplace of the Nation," "A Vacation in Itself," the pier insisted there was "Always a

Tony Grant's children's revue, a Steel Pier perennial, was one of many such productions mounted on Atlantic City stages. Frankie Avalon once took part, as did Andrea McArdle of Broadway's Annie.

George Hamid (left), *who operated
Steel Pier from 1945 through the early
seventies, joined Paul Anka and
unidentified comics. Chimpanzees, it
seemed, were almost always on the pier,
joining Donald O'Connor* (below) *and
Ed McMahon* (opposite).

Good Show," and that its ballrooms, theaters, and arcade were "Always Cool, Clean, and Comfortable." The bottom line: "Nothing Like It Anywhere at Any Price."

It was the first amusement pier in Atlantic City to be built on iron pilings and steel girders. From the day it opened—Saturday, June 18, 1898—Steel Pier was the city's (and probably the world's) largest entertainment center of its kind, sometimes drawing more than a million paying customers a season.

This remarkable success was the result of the efforts of two extraordinary showmen: Frank P. Gravatt, who bought the pier in 1925, and George A. Hamid, who bought it in 1945. Gravatt's shrewd instincts formed the pier's eclectic entertainment policy—opera next-door to vaudeville, next-door to big bands, next-door to news figures who'd show up at a moment's notice. Gertrude Ederle, for instance, was signing autographs on pier within days of her conquest of the English Channel. Her engagement shattered existing attendance records.

For a single admission fee, visitors were able to sample any or all of the attractions. The program of Sunday, July 7, 1928, represents a typical day in the life of Frank Gravatt's Steel Pier: *Il Travatore* (in English); Ronald Colman in *Bulldog*

Ali MacGraw, a contestant in the Prettiest Waitress Contest, 1957.

Drummond—"The Perfect All Talking Picture"; "Presentations and 35 Steel Pier-Ettes, Beautiful Singing and Dancing Girls"; Steel Pier Minstrels; Silent Photoplays; Jack Crawford and His Merry Dance Orchestra; High Diving Horses; Water Sports Carnival; "The Female Human Cannon Ball, *A Girl Shot from a Giant Cannon.*"

When the deed was transferred to the flamboyant Hamid, Steel Pier's reputation spread the world over. His promotion of the pier was matched only by his promotion of himself.

Hamid's special genius was his uncanny ability to anticipate and to satisfy the public's latest whim. He was watchful of the unexpected song, by an unheard-of group, sneaking up the charts. He booked the artists for a weekend on the pier. Consequently, more than a few fast-disappearing acts found their way to Steel Pier billboards, Brooklyn Bridge, for example, or the Doodletown Pipers.

You win some, you lose some. By the time the sixties rolled around, Steel Pier was losing more and more. Names like Hope, Sinatra, Cantor, Burns, and Amos and Andy had given way to names like Funicello, Fabian, Checker, and Danny and the Juniors. In the early seventies, the pier's finger had slipped off the pulse, and the Hamid family bailed out. Then, in 1978, the eighty-year-old wonder passed into the hands of Resorts International, the operator of Atlantic City's first legal casino.

As for starshine, now that Vegas-style gambling has caught on in Atlantic City, you see Vegas-style entertainment. The cast of characters would change again, to names like Rickles, Newton, Humperdinck, and Severinsen, and if that's what it takes to make the America of the eighties laugh, cry, or stomp its feet, so be it. Atlantic City will keep kicking. For the history of show business there is so glorious, so colorful, and so deep, the town simply doesn't know when to quit. Taking a cue from the waves that wash inexorably against Steel Pier's pilings, the show *will* go on.

The Beatles ate a yummy submarine, 1964. Inset, Lyndon Johnson and Danny Thomas at the Democratic Convention, 1964.

The Golden Mermaid Trophy (inset), "awarded annually to America's most beautiful bathing girl," 1921.
Peggy Heavens personified the Golden Mermaid in 1923.

MERMAIDS
ASCENDANT

THE KID HAD WON FIRST PRIZE in a beauty contest. Her picture had been selected by some newspaper editors, and it is said that when a reporter dropped by to interview her, she was shooting marbles outside her home in Washington, D.C. A month or so later, she boarded a train to Atlantic City, there to smile, prance in the sunshine, and compete against seven others in a pageant on the beach.

She is the queen of the girls of the summer. Gaze at her photograph, and you find an unwavering good nature, a sprite whose eyes mask no dark spirit. And as she stands there, in that crazy crown and her string of pearls, she is a sunkissed mermaid in a flag-draped conch.

Margaret Gorman had just turned sixteen, was a little over five feet tall, weighed 108 pounds, had light brown hair and blue eyes, and measured 30-25-32.

She assembled with the others on September 6, 1921. They came from Washington, Pittsburgh, Harrisburg, Ocean City, Newark, New York, Philadelphia, and Atlantic City itself. It is fitting to name names: Misses Gorman, Thelma Matthews, Emma Pharo, Hazel Harris, Margaret Bates, Virginia Lee, Nellie Orr, and Ethel Charles. A hostess committee accompanied them to their rooms at beachfront hotels. That evening they were entertained at the Almanac Restaurant, where each received an Atlantic City scroll presented by Mayor Bader. When dinner was over they went to the Apollo, to watch a vaudeville show from two tiers of boxes reserved just for them. By midnight they were asleep—or trying to be.

Arriving promptly at ten the next morning, King Neptune came ashore from a yacht anchored at sea in front of the Dennis Hotel. He was eighty-year-old Hudson Maxim, described by the Chamber of Commerce as the "world-famous inventor of smokeless gunpowder." He had white hair and a white beard, carried a trident in one hand, and in the other the Golden Mermaid, a resplendent trophy consisting of a sea nymph lying on a wave-streaked rock. He'd later tell pageant officials: "While I am exceedingly strong and rugged …if I were placed next to someone smelling to high heaven with perfume, I'd collapse and fall in a heap." Accordingly, contestants were prohibited from applying any perfume or talc.

Eccentric Neptune led the eight beauties and a gaggle of gawkers to the Keith Vaudeville Theater on Garden Pier. There, the contestants passed before the judges, who included the famed illustrator Howard Chandler Christie, actor John Drew, plus a few artists from Philadelphia and Atlantic City. Little Margaret Gorman stole

Margaret Gorman of Washington, D.C., Miss America, 1921.

their hearts—*and there she was:* Atlantic City's most beautiful Inter-City bathing queen, winner of the Golden Mermaid, and our first Miss America.

Why here? Why did Atlantic City give rise to this pulchritudinous highlight of the American Dream?

It all goes back to the Season. Some kind of post–Labor Day festival had been long talked about by city business leaders, the point being to scratch out another profitable week of Season. They hit upon the Atlantic City Fall Pageant, which included a Bathers Revue, Rolling Chair Parade, Night Spectacle with the Frolique of Neptune, and the Inter-City Beauty Contest. It was a weekend bash with a week's buildup and several day's mop-up.

The Chamber of Commerce kept close watch on the benefits of the pageant of '21. "In the publicity gained for the resort," its newsletter noted, "direct results already are

The Inter-City bathing contestants, 1921. Margaret Gorman (second from left) was the winner, becoming the nation's first Miss America.

being reported throughout the hotel district. Travel from Washington and other cities where the Beauty Contests were conducted…has never been heavier at this time [of year], and there is every reason to believe that the tremendous flood of news and pictures printed throughout the country will bring Atlantic City before the public…in a manner which will be advantageous to the resort."

In a series of impassioned notices to local entrepreneurs, the Chamber pulled out all stops: "Join Up! Be a Wise One! Join Up! Mr. Business Man, Show Your Faith in Your Home City—Make the Pageant a Representative Civic Demonstration."

Entries were solicited for a great procession of rolling chairs and floats, each bearing the name of a hotel, restaurant, store, railroad, or utility.

Word went out to men, women, and children, inviting them to take part in a gigantic bathers' parade along the beach, with honors going to civic and social

After leading a procession along the beach at Garden Pier, Margaret Gorman unsuccessfully defended her crown in 1922.

groups that looked best in bathing suits, to adorable kids under twelve, to men "having the best physical appearance," to anyone who wished to create a "comic or humourously unique bathing costume," to women who weren't "actresses, motion-picture players, or professional swimmers," and to women who were.

All this was just the beginning. The featured attraction was that Inter-City Beauty Contest.

Though limited to only eight contestants, the 1921 Inter-City competition was a box-office bonanza. It was so stunning that fifty-eight beauties showed up the next year, ten from New York State alone. The *Times* devoted days of consecutive coverage to the pageant of 1922. On September 8 it reported: "The nation's picked beauties swept along three miles of Boardwalk this afternoon in the most spectacular rolling-chair parade ever staged here. Crowds packed the borders of the walk,

A souvenir program cover later used on a postcard, 1923.

Mary Kathleen Campbell was the only two-time Miss America, winning in 1922 and 1923. After having taken her hometown title in Columbus, Ohio, Miss Campbell was told that her success was the result of her figure. "What's a figure?" she reportedly asked her mother. "None of your business," her mother replied.

His Oceanic Majesty, King Neptune, presided over the early pageants. Neptune was portrayed by Hudson Maxim, shown here, the inventor of smokeless gunpowder.

squeezed in the windows of the flanking hotels and stores, and kept up a continuous cheering from the time that King Neptune and his flower-bedecked retinue got underway. Airplanes swooped down and showered the bowered beauties with roses and confetti. Cannons roared and even the breakers boomed forth their tribute to America's prettiest girls."

Once more, Neptune was portrayed by the mighty Hudson Maxim, who marched in front, free from any whiff of perfume. "Then followed the 58 representative beauties, 21 brass bands, 2 orchestras, and 250 floats and rolling chairs. In the first division the contestants for the beauty prize, clad in colorful afternoon gowns reclined, almost smothered in clematis, marigold, larkspur, roses, gladioli, and asters."

Margaret Gorman was again on hand, hoping to defend her title. Instead, she wound up crowning her successor, the towering (five feet seven inches) Mary Campbell of Columbus, Ohio. (Miss Campbell would win again in 1923, becoming the first, and last, two-time Miss America.) The judges that year included the sharp-eyed Norman Rockwell, Lee Shubert, and Flo Ziegfeld.

Also in attendance was the seventy-two-year-old president of the American Federation of Labor, Samuel Gompers, who observed unofficially. "I have traveled afar, but this is the greatest treat I was ever afforded," he told the *Times.* "It will be a superhuman task to choose the prettiest, and I am glad I have not the responsibility....To me, however, Miss Washington [Margaret Gorman] most greatly appeals. She represents the type of womanhood America needs—strong, red-blooded, able to shoulder the responsibilities of homemaking and motherhood. It is in her type that the hope of the country rests."

As far as Gompers was concerned—and it was true of many community leaders at the time—the parade of beauties was as American as apple crunch. Watching

Local businessmen sponsored floats that rolled in the pageant's Boardwalk parades, like these from the 1920s.

Ruth Malcomson of Philadelphia, Miss America, 1924. Inset, *Joan "Rosebud" Blondell, Miss Dallas, 1926.*

them go by, you were filled with patriotic stirrings matched only by the sight of smart-stepping Boy Scouts.

Others, however, talked turkey. A reporter for the *Atlantic City Press*, standing elbow to elbow with the esteemed Mr. Gompers, came away with more feverish impressions: "[They were] piquant jazz babies who shook the meanest kind of shoulders, pink-skinned beauties of all types. Tanned athletic girls, bare of limb, shapely of figure and women wearing their water togs gracefully, olive-hued and bejeweled favorites of the harem, stately colonial dames in hoop skirts, mandarin ladies, with black eyes peeping coyly from behind waving fans."

The reporter would be the first to admit: there were better things to do with these women than pledge allegiance to them. But, as we've seen, Atlantic City had always managed to confuse the wholesome with the wholesale, a clean time with a good time. And from its beginning, the Miss America Pageant reflected the paradox.

Lenora Slaughter (left), *in the flowered hat, served as executive secretary of the Miss America Pageant until her retirement in 1967. Three years earlier, Mrs. Slaughter had received the She-Shell Award, presented to the resort's outstanding woman of the year. Albert A. Marks, Jr. (above), chairman of the pageant's executive committee, guided Miss America into the era of television.*

As Frank Deford notes in his entertaining history of the event, *There She Is* (1971): "The pageant manages to mix up its sex with respectable community boosterism."

Certain sticklers found the marriage between beauty and business to be entirely unholy. For instance, the directors of Trenton's YWCA warned of "grave dangers from unscrupulous persons to which the girls are exposed." Charles Funnell quotes them in *By the Beautiful Sea*: "It was noticed by competent observers that the outlook in life of the girls who participated was completely changed. Before the competition they were splendid examples of innocence and pure womanhood. Afterward their heads were filled with vicious ideas."

BUT ENOUGH! Our purpose here is to relax and enjoy, to have a good long gape at the summertime ladies who flocked to the shore, beauties who came to compete not only for America's choicest crown, but for a hundred tiaras: Miss Hydrangea Queen, Miss Beach Patrol, Miss Press Photographer, Miss Submarine, Miss Prettiest

Waitress, Miss Columbus Day, Miss Irish-America, Miss Oriental U.S.A., Miss Queen Esther, Miss United Way, Ms. Senior Citizen, even Miss International Nude.

Still others vied for Miss Mermaid, who each year performed the solemn ceremony of "unlocking" the sea on Memorial Day. Or they came simply because that knew that somebody was *always* looking for a few pretty girls for some nutty reason or another: to dress up as lobsters to advertise a restaurant, to lead Elsie the Cow into the surf as a publicity stunt; to pretend to be fishing off a mechanical elephant for God-knows-what-purpose.

And all around these ladies, the shutters clicked, the bulbs popped. Pictures went out over the wire. Americans everywhere took a gander, not a quick gander either, but a lingering eyeful. Then, on the weekend after Labor Day, came the most famous eyeful of all, as the entire nation squinted, checked its mermaids up and down, training its orbs on Miss America herself. Were those clicks and pops, or were they thunder and lightning?

In the early years of the pageant, looks got you everywhere. Talent? Congeniality? A lifetime pledged to good works and charity? Forget it! All you really

Russell Patterson's rendering of Jean Bartel of California, Miss America 1943.

needed was to rack up more beauty points than the next gal. Mary Campbell, for example, won in '22 and '23 because she scored highest on a scale that awarded fifteen points for the construction of her head; ten for her eyes; five for her hair; five for her nose; five for her mouth; and ten each for her facial expression, torso, legs, arms, hand, and "grace of bearing."

The best-known contestant from the twenties was fifteen-year-old Miss Dallas, a girl called Rosebud who, in 1926, according to her own description in *There She Is*, had "a good, big chest, the kind garbagemen whistle at."

She was named Rosebud Blondell, though she was really Joan Blondell, who wasn't from Dallas at all. She found herself marooned there with her father's penniless vaudeville show. The Dallas contest, you see, carried a cash prize of two thousand dollars, more than enough to bring Ed Blondell and Company back east.

Rosebud—she chose the name because of a part she'd played in a grade school production—swept the Dallas competition and came to Atlantic City. She rode down the Boardwalk on a float decorated with cacti and tumbleweed, twirling a couple of six-shooters, the first time she'd ever held guns in her young life. Rosebud

Caught in a relaxed moment: four contestants from the pageant of 1941.

drawled her way to the semifinals, an experience that gave her a lifelong affection for Atlantic City. In 1929 she returned to play opposite Jimmy Cagney in *Penny Arcade*, and in the fifties, when married to Mike Todd, she visited often, dining at the Marlborough-Blenheim (where Rosebud had stayed).

The city decided to abandon the pageant following the 1927 edition. As Deford points out, the cancellation had little to do with the coming of the Depression—as some would claim—and a lot to do with the fact that the affair had begun to generate bad press. There were rumors of exploitation and bribes, none particularly serious. But from 1928 through 1932, the nation was Missless, though it had more than enough troubles with which to occupy itself.

The pageant returned in '33, on very shaky pins, and without the wholehearted support of city businessmen. The winner that year was Marion Bergeron, Miss Connecticut, who'd go on to make a fair name for herself as a singer with Guy Lombardo's orchestra. After another disappearance in '34, the pageant resurfaced and has been with us ever since, ceremonies taking place on Atlantic City piers until 1940, when the show moved to the gargantuan Convention Hall.

It is doubtful the pageant could have survived without Lenora Slaughter, who

The complete cast, 1948: Actress Vera (Ralston) Miles, Miss Kansas, is second from left, top row. The winner that year was BeBe Shopp, eighth from left, top row.

helped organize its return in 1935 and served as its executive secretary until her retirement in 1967. Tireless, decisive, and wearing velvet gloves over her iron fists, Slaughter was the force that kept things together. Says Deford: "While she has felt almost a crusader's impulse to drag *Miss America* into respectability, [her] initial chore was simply to keep the pageant afloat. In many ways this may have been her greatest feat, seeing as how she was originally threatened by financial disaster on one side and ennui on the other."

Slaughter concerned herself with every last sequin, making sure the events went smoothly, keeping a steely eye on the institution's image.

In the early fifties Slaughter was joined by another who'd held an abiding commitment to pageant ideals, Albert A. Marks, Jr. In 1954, Marks represented the pageant in its first nervous negotiations with television, selling off rights to ABC for ten thousand dollars. The initial Miss America telecast occurred later that year, drawing some twenty-seven million viewers, or an audience share of 39 percent. (Lee Meriweather, Miss California, was the winner.)

In Albert Marks, the pageant had a man supremely adept at guiding it into the television era and the complications thereof. Deford observed that Marks

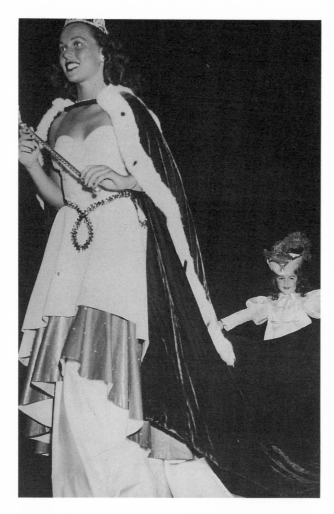

Best of the known faces: Bess Myerson of New York, Miss America, with her page Vicki Gold, 1945.

Cloris Leachman (left), Miss Chicago, 1946.

was singularly effective in preserving the autonomy of the pageant, not allowing networks to dictate controls over the production, as has happened to so many other events. Marks has said: "...I am a great deal more concerned with maintaining our national image than with ratings *per se*, or money. If you take the top dollar, you pay the top price." Accordingly, he has chosen to run the pageant as a nonprofit enterprise, getting sponsors to put their money into scholarship programs and pageant promotion, and giving the networks a reasonable deal in exchange for their noninterference.

Frank Deford's *There She Is* is unquestionably the most definitive look at the Miss America phenomenon. Through conscientious reporting and lively prose, Deford provides some interesting facts about the business.

Item. Bette Cooper, Miss America of 1937, Miss Bertrand Island (N.J.), was so surprised, frightened, and reluctant a winner that she ran off with her escort the night of her victory, refusing to show up for subsequent pageant activities. In effect, she never accepted her crown.

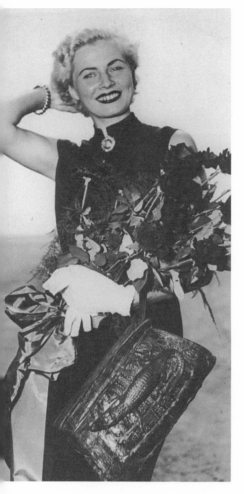

Anita Ekberg, then a big star on the Continent, was invited to be a noncompeting entrant in 1951.

Lee Meriweather of California, Miss America, 1955.

Phyllis George of Texas, Miss America 1970.

Item. Bess Myerson, 1945's Miss America from New York, was probably the most talented of all winners. Her pageant program consisted of "Summertime" played on a flute, and Grieg's Piano Concerto in A Minor. Some months after her victory, Bess appeared as a soloist at Carnegie Hall.

Item. BeBe Shopp, 1948, and Evelyn Ay, 1954, seem to be the most bosomy Miss Americas, each with a bust measurement of thirty-seven inches.

Item. In the talent department, Miss Montana, 1949, was in the middle of an equestrian routine when her palomino slipped and fell into the orchestra pit. Uninjured, she was later voted Miss Congeniality.

Item. Contrary to the popular belief that most winners come from the South, the state with the most points for Miss Americas and runners-up is California. Next in line come Ohio, Pennsylvania, Texas, and New York.

Item. Many contestants for the crown have had funny names. Deford's personal favorites include Claire Spirt, Irmgard Dietel, Ysleta Leissner, Flora Sleeper,

And here he *is, Bert Parks.*   Joan Teets, Jewel Smerage, Alberta Futch, Dusene Vunovich, Louisa Ann Flook, and Dulcie Scripture.

Whatever happened to the girls of summer, where did they all go? To a chosen few—such as Joan Blondell, Bess Myerson, Lee Meriweather, Cloris Leachman (Miss Chicago, 1946), Anita Bryant (Miss Oklahoma and second runner-up, 1959), Mary Ann Mobley (Miss America, 1959), Vera (Ralston) Miles (Miss Kansas, 1948), Phyllis George (Miss America, 1971), the pageant brought lasting celebrity. But for the rest, there was no more than a single, sparkling year in the sun.

Yet year after year, decade after decade, some things remained the same: the smiles, the tears, the singing of "There she is, Miss America / There she is, your ideal," written by Bernie Wayne and first performed at the pageant of '55. Which brings us to the perennial Bert Parks.

Kylene Barker of Virginia, Miss America, 1979.

The toothy one came aboard in 1955, and it is hard to imagine the pageant without him. It is also hard to imagine what he thinks about up there, given his fervor for the proceedings. Several years ago, without cue cards, Parks told a reporter: "I have been amazed—literally fallen over—by some of the choices of the judges. Ten or eleven of them have been ridiculous. And the crowd reaction....Some choices are so unpopular that it seems Ilie Nastase is up there and the crowd is turning on him."

Parks and pageant associates had some of their hairiest moments in the late 1960s, as feminists stormed Convention Hall in protest of the Miss America image and how, they charged, it exploited and distorted womanhood. One of the leaders of the storm, Robin Morgan, who was arrested on the Boardwalk in 1968, went so far as to remark in a recent speech: "It was right here in super tacky Atlantic City that this wave of the [modern] feminist movement was born."

A variety of floats that took part in the pageant's Boardwalk parade during the forties and fifties.

Atlantic City beauty queens came in all sizes, shapes and colors to compete for a variety of crowns. Above, Little Miss America, 1936. Right, two for the glory: Miss Steel Pier, circa 1962.

Miss Prettiest Waitress, 1962 (top left). *Miss International Nude, 1975* (top center). *Ms. Senior Citizen, 1977* (above). *Miss Mermaid* (left), *unlocking the sea on Memorial Day, 1954.*

Publicists thanked heavens for pretty girls as Atlantic City cranked out a never-ending supply of eye-catching photos. Top, Elsie the Cow and friends, 1941. *Center,* fancy models at an appliance trade convention, 1962. *Right,* Atlantic City as a winter paradise, 1978.

Fishing for attention: a Steel Pier publicity photo, 1943.

Protesting women carried signs that proclaimed MISS AMERICA SELLS IT, and dropped brassieres into a fiery ashcan. Bert Parks himself was forced to hole up inside Convention Hall "because the women wouldn't let me out. I had to shower there, dress there, eat there. They even burned me in effigy and screamed once we were on T.V."

But as the seventies rolled on, the shouting diminished and the ratings held up, probably because most American women wanted it that way.

And while some may think that the pictures that fill these pages are inane, unjust, sexist, and intrinsically exploitive, they are nevertheless expressions of a love affair. Atlantic City was in love with the ladies, ulterior motives notwithstanding. And the ladies were in love with Atlantic City.

The romance, you see, began before the crowns were awarded, before Margaret Gorman won first prize in a beauty contest. In 1915, James Huneker observed:

There is in reality no type of American girlhood. When you hear of the summer girl you may be sure that the phrase was invented by the same lazy-minded male who invented the matinee girl. Both exist only on paper. A stroll down the Boardwalk will prove this. Every variety of girl passes you. She is dark haired and red, blond, and brunette. Her nose is long and thin, thick, Grecian or upturned like the petal of a rose. But she is pretty in her undistinguished way....

Beautiful women as beautiful lobsters, a promotion for Hackney's seafood restaurant, circa 1940.

Petunia ascendant at the Boardwalk Baby Parade, 1968.

I am free to confess that the American girls I saw there were more imposing than their male escorts. They did, indeed, lack a certain distinction, and the English you heard fall from their mouths was often dreadful—not dreadful alone because of its slang but because the intonation, pronunciation, and enunciation were so careless, so slipshod, so deadly common. There are sins overheard in most cities. In Atlantic City they salute you with painful emphasis. But what carriage, what light-footed elegance, what perpetual chewing of gum, what a mixture of twangs!

We're with you, James Huneker. Here's a double Brighton Punch to every last one of them.

Celebrants at the opening of the Resorts International Casino, Memorial Day weekend, 1978.

FUNNY MONEY

ATLANTIC CITY SOLD SHELL GAMES BY THE SEASHORE. She was home to the penny-ante hustler and big-time sport. Those who had it figured brought their pipe dreams, con games, and bright ideas to the resort, hoping to cash in. The tourists, see, had short pockets and long arms, which meant there was gold in dem dar dunes. So step right up, folks, we're here to tell you about the pursuit of the almighty sand dollar.

The cash machine was in high register by 1900. Says Charles Funnell in *By the Beautiful Sea*: "The principal shearing of sheep took place in the scores upon scores of small shops which abutted the Boardwalk on the land side. So long as the stroller was not looking at the ocean, he was looking for something for sale."

What *wasn't* for sale? "Racy postcards, 'Genuine Japanese corlypsis landscapes on pearl shells,' coral, Japanese fern seeds, 'Indian' moccasins, Kewpie dolls, Swiss woodcarving, photographs bedizened with gold lacquer, and a heroic device to cut apples open in the shape of a water lily."

You want *schlocky* souvenirs for the folks back home? Have we got souvenirs for you! In 1896 stores on the Boardwalk sold buttons that read "If you love me, grin," or "I am mama's darling, whose darling are you?"

Sixty years later, the buttons were replaced by sweatshirts with MOSCOW UNIVERSITY on the front, and, in the mid-seventies, by monogrammed jogging shorts and a T-shirt on which a man peers into his own pants, the message reading POLISH PEEPING TOM.

Rubber dice, toy slot machines, a shirt with a donkey on which is written I LOST MY A— IN ATLANTIC CITY are now available for the shopper's consideration, along with snowfall paperweights, and baby pants that say I'M A LITTLE CRAPPER FROM ATLANTIC CITY.

Bingo parlors were popular along the walk, were blue-haired ladies entered under signs that said FASCINATION, POKERINO, THRILL-O. Ed McMahon's father operated one such bingo establishment. At closing time he stuffed the day's receipts into Ed's carriage, then wheeled baby and bread to the Traymore Hotel, where the money was put in a safe. McMahon recalled in his autobiography, *Here's Ed:* "They pushed me along the Boardwalk, late at night, feeling perfectly secure because in those days no one was about to rip off a baby."

Young McMahon got his start in show business on the Boardwalk (as did Jack Klugman, even Charles Bronson, of all people). For a couple of summers, Ed

Below, *a recording studio in which visitors in 1942 warbled for their friends, or enemies, back home. Gadgets of every description were sold to vacationers. Some of them, such as this pants presser demonstrated in 1942 (right), were actually useful.*

worked as a pitchman, demonstrating and selling kitchen gadgets that sliced, diced, chopped, minced, and did just about everything else to your vegetables but eat them.

Then there were the auction houses, where lucky tourists outbid one another on a variety of "steals," though who was stealing from whom was a question that never got answered. The *New York Times*, reporting on the Atlantic City of 1928, noted that "the auctioneers are working hard. Some of them, so they assure their audiences, are giving away valuable goods just to get things started. Someone seems skeptical and gets reprimanded for his lack of confidence in human nature."

Served him right, the cynic. Some people don't know a good deal when they hear one, like the spiel delivered in 1971: "These are real nylon toothbrushes. Each one has exactly 3,419 bristles. If you don't believe me, taken one home and count 'em. They sell at the drugstore for 39 cents. Who will pay a dollar for one? That's all right, I just wanted to see if you're paying attention. Take one free, mister. And you, too, lady. Oh, I've got a lot of free things to give away today...."

"Zippo-type" lighters, back scratchers, combs, and matches showered the audience, pennies from heaven, as auctioneers worked their fever. Then the "valuable pieces" were unwrapped: clocks, radios, lamps, sewing machines. Certain pitchmen, Archie Morris, for instance, became Boardwalk legends. It was the stuff of which classic American salesmanship was made, a technique that sold "the sizzle, not the steak," as *Business Week* has described it.

Other enterprises had a distinctly foreign flavor. George Kato, a first-generation Japanese born in Atlantic City during World War I, remembers his family's penny arcade: "When my father saw Absecon Island, with all its sand dunes and things, he became very homesick. He began to think about Sakanoshima, which was a small island, but of course it had no Boardwalk.... He opened a small business, which was the forerunner of our present day pinball [arcade]."

Nickel-and-dime stuff: the selling of souvenirs has always been one of Atlantic City's leading industries. This shop was on Steel Pier in the early forties. Large buttons read TO HELL WITH HITLER.

Irene's, a souvenir super-market on the Boardwalk for many years.

[It had] a rolling ball, or pingpong game, ten balls for a nickel. It was laid out much like a bowling alley. Instead of pins, there were holes. You got ten balls, and you rolled them on a long table, and you accumulated scores which got you little Made-in-Japan trinkets and prizes. If you stayed for the season, you could accumulate [enough] to acquire a tea set, which in those days was highly prized. A Japanese tea set. Many people, even today, recall their grandmother having a Japanese tea set...up in the attic. Where did it come from? Those pingpong games.

Atlantic City was tea sets, bric-a-brac, knick knacks, and *tchotchkes*—giant pencils with the Atlantic City skyline painted on; jumbo cigars that only the most daring conventioneers could smoke; beach towels that said, WANNA PLAY? It was stuff you'd never buy back home, but somehow you shelled out in Atlantic City.

THERE WAS ALSO a higher grade of commerce. Atlantic City was in some ways a permanent world's fair, an exposition of technological achievement, a glorification of America's quality of life. For decades, model-home exhibits drew Boardwalk crowds, as tourists entered tomorrow's kitchen as if they were entering a cathedral. All-electric living. Appliances that did everything but walk the dog. At Steel Pier, General Motors displayed its latest cars, and whenever there was a civic celebration, companies such as General Electric would donate something grand, like the world's biggest light bulb.

In 1929, just months before the U.S. economy sputtered and crashed, the *New York Times* said that Atlantic City "is the America of the national advertising page, of the automobile, of the radio, of the motion pictures." And of the Boardwalk it

said: "[It] is magnificent proof of America's newly found wealth and leisure. It is an iridescent bubble on the surface of our fabulous prosperity."

Certain shopkeepers championed the image. Reese Palley, for one, called himself "Merchant to the Rich" and priced his goods accordingly. Palley's Boardwalk gift shop, established in 1956, sold Boehm birds, LeBeau diamonds, Meissen ceramics, Royal Worcester china, and knock-offs of Tiffany lamps. As Joan Kron described him in an article for *Philadelphia* magazine: "He's...a reconstituted blend of P. T. Barnum and Mike Todd, seasoned to taste like Bernard Berenson."

But Captain John L. Young gets the nod as Atlantic City's king of conspicuous consumption. Young, who built amusement piers, fished with Thomas Edison,

Reese Palley—self-described as "Merchant to the Rich"— is the king of Boehm birds, china, and ceramics.

Visitors emptied their pockets to win things they wouldn't dream of buying. Above, a typical game of skill. Below, a Boardwalk bingo parlor.

Famed auctioneer Archie Morris offered a nonstop pitch to lure customers to his Boardwalk stand, 1972.

and amassed a fortune at the resort, lived out his days at No. 1 Atlantic Ocean, a three-story Venetian palace smack in the middle of Young's Million Dollar Pier. It was an alabaster villa surrounded by formal gardens and a vegetable patch, furnished with crystal chandeliers imported from Austria, and massive tables and chairs—in the shape of marine life and seashells—that were custom made in Venice, Italy, Europe.

Built in 1908, No. 1 Atlantic Ocean had marble statuary in its gardens, including eight-foot likenesses of Adam and Eve. Inside and out, the house was bathed in pastel lights, the effects worked out by Edison himself. Yet amidst all this splendor, Captain and Mrs. Young espoused homespun virtues. He would remark on how nice it was to fish from his bedroom window; she liked to say that she hardly ever needed to dust.

Young's empire was built on the pennies, nickels, and dimes handed over by eager tourists. Other fortunes were made less innocently. Atlantic City, it need be stressed, was wild and crazy for much of its youth, a place they called wide open. Prostitution, rumrunning, and illegal gambling were the principal vices, with authorities averting their eyes.

As early as 1890, liquor licenses passed from one palm to the next. Gaming rooms could be found block after block—from the nickel-limit joints on Mississippi Avenue to the Delaware Avenue club called Dutchy's, "where some of the best known politicians and…businessmen of Philadelphia stake their five and ten dollars on the deal," the *Philadelphia Bulletin* reported.

The newspaper, which at the time was conducting a moral crusade against the resort, went on to list the addresses of twenty-four popular brothels, including

Atlantic City was a permanent world's fair, exhibiting the homes of tomorrow, technological achievements, and a blue-sky version of everyday life, such as this display of 1938.

May Woodston's "pestilential hole" and a cathouse called the Sea Breeze, operated by Minnie Wiegle, "the high kicker in Fox's Theatre fifteen years ago."

Moreover, according to Charles Funnell, "the vice industry was not confined strictly to whites in Atlantic City. Charles Colman kept a gambling house for blacks on Arkansas Avenue, whose crap games were particularly frequented by hotel waiters." On Arctic there was an interracial brothel run by a black madam with a white husband, and the *Daily Union* spoke of a W. H. Furney, who was allowed to conduct his "low negro resort" (at Baltic and North Carolina) because he was adept at turning out the black vote on election days.

With the onset of Prohibition, Atlantic City became one of the East Coast's most notorious seaports. Rumrunning was a major growth industry, as speedboats—loaded to the gunwales—outraced the Coast Guard in nightly forays. Leslie Kammerman, an Atlantic City resident, remembers the scene on Carson Avenue,

a small street overlooking the bays on the north side of town: "Alongside my house there was a railway constructed specifically and solely for [the cargo] of the high-speed boats…. As a little tot, my older brothers used to show me the machine gun slugs that sometimes lodged in the wooden framework of these boats…. The Coast Guard officers would speak to the rumrunners, joke about shooting at each other the night before."

When it came to nabbing bootleggers, Atlantic City law enforcers were often out to lunch. Another city resident recalls: "A well known detective lived down the street from us, and I was very friendly with his son. Every once in a while I would get together with the son, and the detective would take us to the President Hotel, where we would go down to the beach…in our bare feet, wade out into the water and pick up burlap bags. There were always two of them, and we'd put them in the car and take them home. This was the little payoff…. The rumrunners

No. 1 Atlantic Ocean, Captain John Young's home on Million Dollar Pier. The villa was built in 1908 of imported marble. Thomas Edison designed the pastel lighting that bathed the house and sculpture garden. Inset, Captain Young (left) in the sculpture garden, circa 1921.

Atlantic City, particularly the Gardner's Basin region near the Inlet, was a principal East Coast port of entry for Prohibition bootleggers. Coast Guard vessels chased the rumrunners across Atlantic City's bays, sometimes nabbing crew and cargo, sometimes not. This 1929 photograph shows a boat that didn't get away.

would drop them off in the water, and they'd wash ashore. I suppose I was a rumrunner too, just carting them back to the car."

While much of the bootlegged liquor was transported elsewhere, a great many bottles were delivered to Atlantic City nightspots, such as Daniel Garfield Stebbins' Golden Inn at Mississippi and Pacific. Gloria Valleé, Stebbins grandniece, recalled in the *Atlantic City Press:* "Uncle Dan, like all the others, got his liquor from the runners. The ships brought it from Scotland, or South America, and docked at the three-mile limit off Brigantine. The runners, in boats painted gray and completely darkened, would go out to meet the ships, pick up the liquor and sell it to the clubs."

In 1927, Dan Stebbins married a show girl named Blanche Babbitt, from Waynesburg, Pennsylvania, and the Golden Inn was rechristened Babette's, after Blanche's adopted stage name. The club prospered for twenty years, known for the charcoaled steaks served in its dining room, for the stars who appeared on its stage (Eleanor Powell, Joe Penner, and Milton Berle, among others), and for the

club's back room, scene of some of Atlantic City's hottest gambling action. At Babette's, as well as at other posh dens like the old 500 Club and the Bath and Turf Club, horseplayers, cardplayers, and high rollers of every persuasion hob-nobbed with the Vanderbilts, the Astors, and political figures. Illegal though they were, Atlantic City's back rooms were the worst-kept secrets in town.

Oh, there was the occasional raid. In 1943, for instance, Sheriff James Carmack led an attack on Babette's, arresting Stebbins and eight others, seizing racing sheets, crap tables, roulette wheels, and telephones. For Stebbins, the action caused more inconvenience than anything else: he was fined five thousand dollars and was back in business in no time.

Illegal betting and other forms of vice flourished in Atlantic City for a variety of reasons. The town's political and law enforcement bureaucracies either ignored the goings-on, or actively abetted them. Some city officials profited handsomely

The bar at Babette's, 1947, a nightclub and gambling den that catered to out-of-town society. Blanche Babbitt (inset) came to the shore from a small town in Pennsylvania and married Dan Stebbins, who named his joint Babette's in honor of Blanche's stage name. Stebbins died in 1960, Blanche in 1963.

The Bath and Turf Club near the Boardwalk was for years a thriving illegal gambling spot. On August 9, 1958—when these pictures were taken—the club was raided by police and shut down. Forty-four were arrested and nineteen thousand dollars seized.

from payoffs and bribes. Additionally, there was the unspoken assumption that a wide-open city was attractive to tourists.

Thus it is that Atlantic City old-timers smile when asked how casino gambling will change their town. The fact is, Atlantic City has long been a bettor's paradise, less publicized than it is today, certainly less legal, but where there has never been a shortage of frantic action.

For over thirty years, the main link between Atlantic City's political arena and its sporting life was GOP boss Enoch L. "Nucky" Johnson, officially the treasurer of Atlantic County, unofficially the "Beau Brummel of the Ritz-Carlton," friend to show people, mobsters, politicos, and assorted characters beyond Damon Runyon's wildest imagination.

Nucky entered politics in 1904, when he was put on the public payroll by his father, then sheriff of the county. Seven years later Nucky had achieved considerable clout, controlling patronage, proposing or blocking legislation, cutting through municipal red tape on behalf of friends, or tying up enemies in same. A carnation always in his lapel, Nucky attended every important theater opening and gala, and was a denizen of Atlantic City's most fashionable watering holes.

"Atlantic City was the jewel of his domain," wrote a *Reader's Digest* muckraker in 1941. "Visitors on holiday are [Atlantic City's] chief means of livelihood, and even its staid citizens agreed that any taint of puritanism would painfully shrivel the crowds on the Boardwalk.... There were two big businesses in this famous resort— the hotels and the rackets. The rackets were the bigger. Gambling, the red light district, and minor rackets grossed $10,000,000 a year.

"Of this, $250,000 a year went to Nucky. Every cop held his job through Johnson. The sheriff who personally supervised the choosing of jury panels was his brother Al. Enoch L. Johnson Booster Clubs in every precinct delivered half of the county's votes. It was the perfect setup."

Enoch "Nucky" Johnson (left) had little trouble getting guests to turn out for his birthday parties. He entered the political scene in 1904 and was to rule Atlantic City until 1941. Nucky Johnson (inset, right) strolled the Boardwalk with Al Capone (center) during a convention of high-level mobsters, 1929.

The setup enabled government T-men to enjoy a great number of visits to Atlantic City. They came on May 14, 1929, to observe a business convention attended by underworld heavies Frank Costello, Meyer Lansky, Lucky Luciano, Dutch Schultz, Louis "Lepke" Buchalter, and Al Capone. Nucky Johnson, the perfect host, served up steaks, whisky, entertainment, and beautiful women to help the conventioneers relax after a busy day. There were simpler pleasures as well. One writer noted that "rest periods found the gangsters strolling along the beach with their trousers rolled up around their knees, their shoes and socks in their hands, their feet washed by the lapping surf of the Atlantic Ocean."

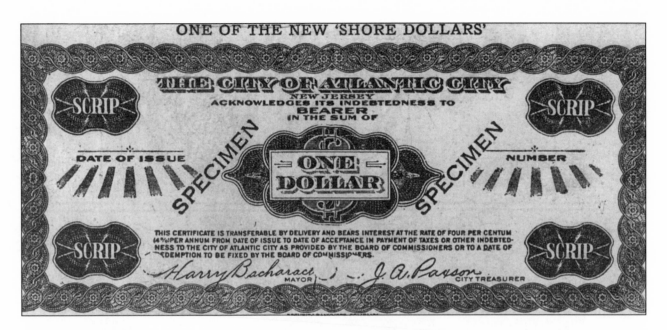

ONE OF THE NEW 'SHORE DOLLARS'

THE CITY OF ATLANTIC CITY
NEW JERSEY
ACKNOWLEDGES ITS INDEBTEDNESS TO
BEARER
IN THE SUM OF

SCRIP

DATE OF ISSUE

ONE DOLLAR

NUMBER

SPECIMEN

SPECIMEN

SCRIP

SCRIP

SCRIP

THIS CERTIFICATE IS TRANSFERABLE BY DELIVERY AND BEARS INTEREST AT THE RATE OF FOUR PER CENTUM (4%)PER ANNUM FROM DATE OF ISSUE TO DATE OF ACCEPTANCE IN PAYMENT OF TAXES OR OTHER INDEBTEDNESS TO THE CITY OF ATLANTIC CITY AS PROVIDED BY THE BOARD OF COMMISSIONERS OR TO A DATE OF REDEMPTION TO BE FIXED BY THE BOARD OF COMMISSIONERS.

Harry Bacharach
MAYOR

J. A. Parson
CITY TREASURER

The city issued municipal scrip in 1933, when the depression nearly wiped out the resort. About $9,500,000 worth of relatively worthless money was circulated.

One of the decisions reached at the conference was that Capone take the heat off the mob by agreeing to a short jail sentence. Dutifully, Scarface went directly from the shore to Philadelphia, where he gave himself up on a gun-possession charge, receiving a one-year sentence.

Perhaps the medical quacks were right about the soothing effect of the Atlantic City air. When turning himself in, Capone said: "I'm tired of gang murders and gang shootings. I'm willing to live and let live. I have a wife and an eleven-year-old boy in Florida. If I could go there and forget it all, I'd be the happiest man in the world. It was with the idea of making peace amongst the gangsters that I spent the week in Atlantic City and got the word of each leader that there will be no more shooting."

Much of Atlantic City's funny money turned to dust in the Crash of '29. Hotels sat empty, nightclubs closed, the Boardwalk was a crown with its diamonds missing. In the absence of real money, a different kind of currency was issued during the Depression: play money. In 1933, the city was so broke it failed to meet its own payroll, and city council was forced to distribute scrip, certificates to be redeemed for dollars when conditions permitted.

Frank Havens, the chief city photographer, remembers those dark days of the early thirties: "Scrip at that time was worth very little, and storekeepers were reluctant to take it…. Eventually, you began to get more for your scrip: first fifty cents on the dollar, seventy-five, then eighty-five. But you were usually tied to a particular grocery store, where you'd deal on credit. And they had you because it was the only place that would take your scrip. So they were always raising their prices."

In the years before recovery, the city issued $9,483,000 worth of municipal play money, all of which was eventually redeemed except for the $100,000 that remained in the hands of souvenir collectors.

ANOTHER FORM OF PLAY money was issued in far greater amounts. MONOPOLY money. Its first minting was not in Atlantic City but in the Germantown

Charles Darrow, inventor of MONOPOLY, was a Philadelphian who often visited Atlantic City, naming the game's streets after those at the shore.

Landing on Atlantic City: the streets of the resort are not really painted red, green, yellow, and orange, nor is there much free parking. These photographs show what certain MONOPOLY landmarks looked like throughout history.

Clockwise from upper right:
Kentucky Avenue, 1913;
Boardwalk, 1935;
Pennsylvania Avenue, 1934;
Atlantic Avenue, 1927;
the Electric Company, 1938;
Park Place, 1931;
Virginia Avenue, 1944;
Jail, 1969.

197

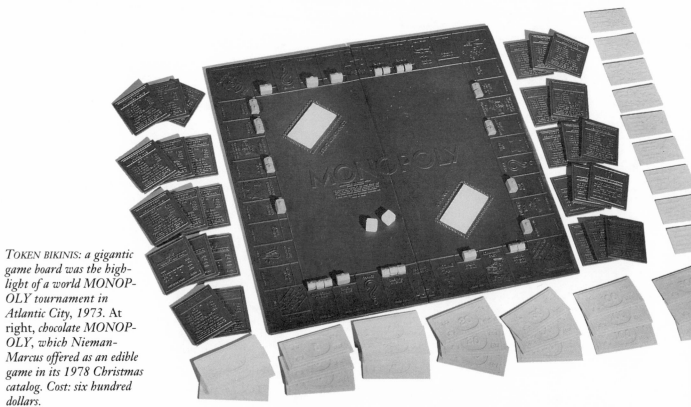

TOKEN BIKINIS: a gigantic game board was the highlight of a world MONOPOLY tournament in Atlantic City, 1973. At right, chocolate MONOPOLY, which Nieman-Marcus offered as an edible game in its 1978 Christmas catalog. Cost: six hundred dollars.

MONOPOLY MADNESS: four students in California played forty-four consecutive days underwater in 1975.

section of Philadelphia, where unemployed salesman Charles Darrow lived with his wife and child, struggling to make ends meet.

According to Maxine Brady's *MONOPOLY Book* (1974), Darrow sat down at his kitchen table one night in 1930 and devised a board game based on the buying and selling of real estate. Properties were named for streets Darrow knew from his many vacations in Atlantic City, streets that meet the Boardwalk from the inlet to Park Place. When he found himself one street short, according to Brady, he selected a little-known section of Margate, a neighboring community, misspelling Marven Gardens as *Marvin* Gardens. There was another small cheat. Darrow needed a fourth railroad to go with the three railway lines that serviced the shore at the time. So he slipped in the Short Line which was, in truth, a bus company.

Darrow failed in his first attempt to sell MONOPOLY to Parker Brothers. Edward P. Parker has said that he liked the game well enough, but felt "it violated several…elementary rules for a family game. We felt that forty-five minutes was about the right length of time for a game, but MONOPOLY could go on for hours. Also, a game is supposed to have a definite end somewhere. In MONOPOLY you kept going around and around. The rules involving mortgages and rents seemed much too complicated. The decision [in 1934] to turn it down was unanimous."

Ever determined, Darrow made up a few thousand sets and sold them to Philadelphia department stores, where they were snapped up. Hearing of the success, Parker Brothers offered the inventor a royalty deal, on the condition that

Birth of a casino: the first hotel with legal gambling, Resorts International, was formerly the Chalfonte-Haddon Hall, shown here in 1904. Inset, an early hotel limousine.

Haddon Hall, shortly before the roof sign was changed to Resorts International. Extensive interior renovations were made leading up to the casino's opening in 1978. Above, the hotel's present linousine.

the company could make certain rules changes. Darrow agreed and, in the tradition of the game itself, retired to a life of riches.

MONOPOLY, of course, became one of the best-selling games in history. Parker Brothers reports proudly that it has manufactured over *3.5 billion* little green houses, that the game is marketed in eighty countries, though the Atlantic City locations are usually changed to suit the territory. For example, Boardwalk becomes Mayfair in England, Rue de la Paix in France, Paseo del Prado in Spain.

In 1973, as talk of casino gambling grew in Atlantic City, the public works commissioner suggested that the resort spruce itself up by revising some of its street signs. Baltic and Mediterranean were avenues that changed names as they wound through town. Commissioner Arthur W. Ponzio proposed that each be known by a single name: the route that was partially known as Baltic would become Fairmont, Mediterranean would become Melrose. Ponzio caught it from all sides. Hundreds of protesters, MONOPOLY fanatics, showed up for the hearing at which the proposal was up for discussion. According to Brady's book, an *ad hoc* committee of Princeton students issued a statement: "The streets of Atlantic City, through the medium of MONOPOLY, have been a microcosm of life in which Baltic and Mediterranean have represented the last resort of the underdog to hold out against the oppressive forces of Boardwalk and Park Place powermongers."

The proposal was vetoed unanimously by city officials. When the applause faded, Commissioner Joseph Lazarow read the few lines he'd composed for the occasion:

> *To this ordinance vote no.*
> *To our residents it presents a great woe.*
> *Baltic and Mediterranean are the*
> *streets we know.*
> *Without them we could never pass Go.*

(MONOPOLY traditionalists were spared another showdown in 1978, when Parker Brothers stated flatly that the board would not be revised to include properties named after casinos.)

THE DEPRESSION OVER, Atlantic City enjoyed a few more funny-money years, as the town returned to its wicked ways.

On July 14, 1941, the jig was up for Nucky Johnson. Following a painstaking, five-year investigation by treasury agents, Nucky was convicted of tax evasion. He was fined twenty thousand dollars and sentenced to ten years at Lewisburg Prison. Paroled in 1945, he returned to Atlantic City, where he lived quietly until his death in 1968 at the age of eighty-five. (Johnson's mantle was inherited by Frank "Hap" Farley, who, for the next thirty years, served as Atlantic City's political strongman. In the early 1970s, Farley's regime was rocked by political scandals, and Farley was defeated in his bid for reelection to the state senate.)

The war clouds gathered, the Army moved in, and by the time the fifties rolled around, the city was in deep trouble. More and more tourists were jetting to Florida. The dice were not rolling in favor of the "Gay Dowager," as Atlantic City was frequently called throughout these years.

Top, *New Jersey Governor Brendand Byrne opened Atlantic City's first legal casino at 10 A.M., May 27, 1978*. Right, *opening-day crowds, 1978*.

The decline did not come as a surprise. As early as 1936, city leaders searched for a way to reverse the erosion. On February 18, the *New York Times* printed a story under the headline,

ATLANTIC CITY PLANS FOR A SUPER RESORT

EXCLUSIVE CABANA COLONY DISCUSSED AS PART OF A 25-YEAR PROGRAM

The prophetic article read:

Plans to make Atlantic City a "super" resort and one of the leading seashore amusement centers of the world are being made by city officials, civic leaders and business groups, it was disclosed here today.

The plans provide for the mapping of a program which might take twenty-five years to complete and eventually result in the construction of a "Monte Carlo," with recreational divisions for all classes of persons....

One of the most important projects considered is an exclusive cabaña colony for wealthy visitors. On a well-kept section of the waterfront would be erected fine lounging salons and individual cabañas. These would be operated in conjunction with the more exclusive hotels at the resort.

In the same group the "Monte Carlo" would be operated, if and when gambling becomes legal in the state. It is the hope of Mayor White that a horseracing track might be built eventually....

"'Segregation' is not a fair description of our plans," the Mayor said, "but we feel that when groups come here, some seeking rest and quiet, others hilariously

Opening-day action, 1978.

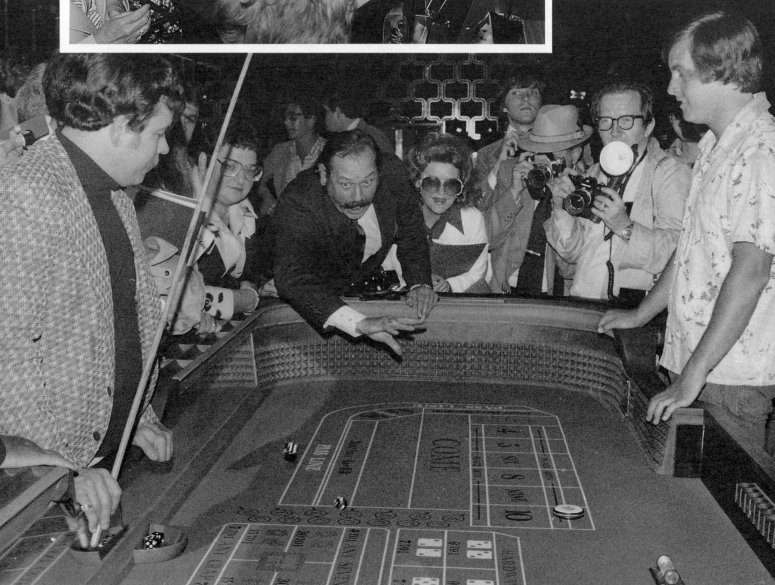

MERMAIDS DESCENDANT: show girls at Resorts International, 1978.

celebrating a hurried holiday, it is absurd to have them trampling on each other's toes and spoiling each other's fun. There should be facilities for every person—and every desire—in Atlantic City. And if visitors want merry-go-rounds or a gambling casino, Atlantic City should give them what they want."

While Atlantic City wouldn't have to wait long for its racetrack, fulfillment of the Monte Carlo dream would stretch beyond Mayor White's twenty-five-year plan. In the meantime, Atlantic City eroded. For a while, it looked like the town might slip back into the desolation called *Absegami*.

By 1970 the Atlantic City tourist was invariably poor, black, elderly, or all three, as described by *Time*. The magazine quoted a third-rate comedian playing the resort: "This town really swings. Every Friday night we shop till ten at the supermarket. Listen, the typical couple visiting Atlantic City these days is a very old lady…and her mother."

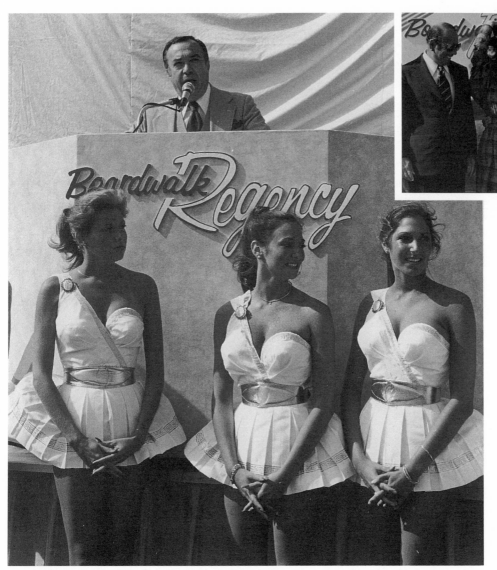

FUTURE MONEY: Ann-Margret (above) *appeared in September 1978 to help Caesars World break ground for its Boardwalk Regency Hotel, scheduled to open Memorial Day, 1979. Atlantic City Mayor Joseph Lazarow* (left) *welcomed Caesars Las Vegas contingent.*

In the seventies the town's poverty rate was the highest in New Jersey. The crime rate was the highest in the nation for a city its size. The population, which had begun to decline as far back as 1940, shrank even more. Atlantic City had three choices: to seek a last-ditch panacea called casino gambling; to become a retirement community financed by social security, welfare, and Medicare; or, failing these, to face near-total extinction.

A referendum calling for the legalization of casino gambling was placed on the state ballot in 1974. It was defeated. In 1976, a similar referendum passed. Let it be heard: the town that had invested a dozen decades pursuing funny money wasn't going to fold without playing its ace.

SATURDAY, MAY 27, 1978. The *Atlantic City Press* ran a banner across its front page: QUEEN OF RESORTS REIGNS AGAIN. "It's here," the story began. "The wheels are spinning and the dice are rolling and the coins are clinking and the grande old dame Atlantic City has a saucy swivel in her hips...

CASINO CITY BY THE SEA: Clockwise, *The Grand, A Bally's Casino Resort, TropWorld Casino and Entertainmet Resort, Trump Plaza Hotel and Casino, Caesars Atlantic City Hotel and Casino, Bally's Park Place Casino and Tower, Claridge Casino Hotel.*

Sands Hotel and Casino, Merv Griffin's Resorts Casino Hotel, Trump Taj Mahal Casino Resort, Showboat Casino and Hotel, Trump's Castle Casino Resort, Harrah's Casino Hotel.

"The city will never be the same again.

"Resorts International Casino opened its doors shortly after 10 A.M Friday and there was a crush of bodies waiting."

The scene was the renovated Chalfonte-Haddon Hall, the ancient Quaker-owned hotel that once refused to sell drinks on the premises. Resorts International spent fifty million to refurbish the place; in the first six months of operation, the casino raked in ten million more than that.

Three hundred thousand people came to Atlantic City that weekend. "It's a new era," said one of them, a man from Washington, D.C. "I like being part of it."

"I see this reawakening Atlantic City," said Joseph Lordi, chairman of the New Jersey Casino Control Commission. "From this day on, I think we will see a city of growth and prosperity."

"I think we have committed ourselves to keeping this as a wholesome family resort," said Mayor Joseph Lazarow. "While still having gambling."

And as he cut the ribbon to open the casino, New Jersey Governor Brendan Byrne said quietly, "My father once told me never to bet on anything but Notre Dame and the Yankees."

With the legalization of gambling, hotels, stores, and piers along the Boardwalk changed hands like deeds in a MONOPOLY game. Out-of-town operators came, saw, and invested in Atlantic City, including Caesars World, Bally Corporation, Playboy, Penthouse, the Golden Nugget, Benihana of Tokyo, Holiday Inn, Ramada Inn, Del Webb, Donald Trump, Merv Griffin, and others. Funny money flew furiously.

At this writing, Atlantic City is going 'round and 'round, and where she will stop is anybody's guess. Will she soar through the ozone, or will she flop? Old nemesis Miami Beach is looking at casino gambling, as are other locations dangerously close to the Queen of Resorts. Will gambling be, as the singer sings in the casino lounge, too much, too little, too late—or will it be Atlantic City's salvation?

Atlantic City today is at the crossroads to somewhere, a city built on hope. There have been over 125 years to explain why she is where she is, a history to reveal how she got here.

Her future rides on a roll of the dice, for when the betting was opened Atlantic City was nowhere: some ancient buildings, a few old people, a memory cooled by ocean breezes.

But take another walk on that everlasting Boardwalk, and you know damn well: somehow the dame can't lose.

PICTURE CREDITS

PHOTOGRAPHERS AND ILLUSTRATORS:

Atlantic City Commercial Photo Co.: 33 top

Atlantic Foto Service: 38, 49, 92, 120 bottom, 152 top, 196 center left

Mike Blizzard: 72 bottom left, 138 top center, 170

C. Bonfort: 121 right

Jack Boucher: 71, 196-97 circle

B. Vartan Boyajian: 200 bottom right, 202 top, 204

Jack Bradley: 139 bottom right, 138 top left

Central Studios: 32 top and center, 41 top and bottom right, 56 top, 61, 73 left, 88 inset, 105 top, 125 top right, 131 center, 132 top right, 140, 142 center left and bottom, 144, 145 top, 162 left, 176 top, 182, 183, 188, 196 top left, 197 bottom, 200 bottom left

Charles Doble, Sr.: 60 bottom, 126 top left and right, 127, 147, 173 top, 178

Esquire Photography: 81, 148, 149

Stanley Gale: 175 top left

Al Gold: 16, 31 top, 35, 63 top, 66 right, 132 top left and circle, 134, 141, 166-67, 168 left

Mark Haven: 180, 184, 186, 202 bottom, 203 top

Frank Havens: 65, 106-107, 132 bottom right, 150, 151 inset, 169, 173 bottom, 179

Hess Photography, Atlantic City: 23 top, 24, 26-27, 32 bottom, 33 center and bottom, 36 bottom left, 37 inset, 41 center left, 44-45 gutter, 54, 62, 73 inset, 77, 80, 94, 104 center and bottom, 105 bottom, 110, 118, 132 top, 146 top, 156-57, 159, 160-61, 175 top center, 177, 189 inset, 196 bottom, 196-97 gutter, 197 center right, 203 bottom

Helen Harding Hunter: 121 left

James Kollar: 137 top

Bud Lee: 113

Mitchell Studio: 120 top right

Mosley: 88-89

Geo. A. McKeague: 84

Lou Ortzman: 169 right, 176 bottom, 198 top

Palace Studio: 22 bottom

Russell Patterson (Illustration): 164

Vincent Guy Sanborn: 57

Sid Shrier: 118

Leo Shumsky Studio: 139 top

H. B. Smith: 34, 197 top right

Robert David Stern: 185

Syd Stoen: 100 top, 138 top right

Strand Studio: 122 bottom

Kelso Taylor: 60 top and bottom, 56 bottom, 76

COLLECTORS:

Harold P. Abrams: 136 top, 137 top

Actors Fund Home: 124 bottom right

Nelson Amey: 56 top, 61, 125 top right, 132 top right, 142 center left, 144

Atlantic City Convention Bureau: 45 bottom right

Atlantic City Free Library: 7, 9 bottom inset, 59, 108 center, 126 bottom right, 123 inset

Atlantic City Press Bureau: 13, 16, 18 bottom, 31 top, 35, 48, 63 top, 65, 66 inset, 74 right, 75 circle, 101 bottom, 105 top, 106-7, 132 top left, circle and bottom right, 141, 150, 151 inset, 166-67, 169 center and right, 173 bottom, 175 top left, 176 bottom, 179, 187, 198 top, 200 center left

Atlantic County Historical Society: x, 18 top, 22 top

Atlantic Electric: 2, 4, 14 top, 21, 73 full page, 196 center left

Burt Bacharach: 133

Nancy and Benjamin Bacharach: 94

Baly's Park Place Casino and Tower: 206

Douglas Beaupit: 81

Boardwalk Regency Hotel: 205 top

Joseph Broski: 24 top and bottom, 33 center and bottom, 152 bottom, 159, 160, 161 top, 189 inset

Walter J. Buzby: 36 center, inset, bottom left and right

Caesars Atlantic City Hotel and Casino: 206

Max Chasens: 112 bottom

Claridge Casino Hotel: 206

Michael Cohen: 5, 28 inset, 44 bottom center, 196 top left

Columbia Pictures: 129 left and right

Chris Columbo: 91, 136 bottom, 137 bottom

Margaret Price Cornell: 120 top right

Faith and Pat Crowe: 57, 138 top left

Paul "Skinny" D'Amato: 140

Willy D'Amato: 131 top, 138 bottom, 139 bottom center

Dolores Friedman Danska: 86, 109 center

Susan Subtle Dintenfass: 113

Margaret and Charles Doble, Jr.: 60 bottom, 126 top left and right, 127, 147, 173 top, 178

John Dollard: 158 left

Frank Driggs Collection: 130 bottom, 131 top and bottom

Chip Dunn: 20

Edison National Historic Site: 40 circle

Mildred Fox: 41 center left, 45 center, 100 top, 104 bottom, 112 top

Fralinger's, Inc.: 12, 30 top right inset

Arnette and Jake French: 30 top left inset, 32 center, 56 bottom, 60 top and bottom, 67 bottom, 76, 79 top right, 142 circle

Jean Godfrey: 191 inset

Beverly Gold: v

Grand, A Bally's Casino Resort, The: 206

Frank Gravatt: 46-47, 78 top, 143

Greater Chamber of Commerce of Atlantic City: 64 bottom right

Harrah's Casino Hotel: 207

Heinz U.S.A.: 26-27, 28 top, 29

Joseph Hackney: 66 right, 146 top

Marion Hackney: 79 bottom, 148 bottom

Jeanette Hall: 88-89

Hamid Enterprises: 32 top and bottom, 54, 84 inset, 103 bottom, 142 bottom, 146 top and bottom, 147, 148 top, 149, 172 bottom, 174 bottom, 176 top, 177, 182, 183, 188

Mr. and Mrs. Edward Harris: 100 bottom

Historical American Buildings Survey: 72 top, 196-97 circle

Historical Society of Pennsylvania: 18 center, 31 bottom, 39 full page, 40 bottom, 70 top, 79 top left, 109 top, 135, 155, 165, 172 top, 174 top, 194

Edward Hitzel: 33 top

E. H. Huber: 104 center

James Kenny: 145 top

Bernie Klempfner (Club Harlem advertising insert): 136

Anthony J. Kutschera: 34, all postcards in Chapter 4

Frankie Laine: 64 top and insert

Ring Lardner, Jr.: 124 top

Vicki Gold Levi: 3, 23 top, 30 bottom, 37 inset, 38 full page, 44 top, 62, 73 inset, 77, 78, 80, 92, 103 top, 110, 134, 156-57, 161 bottom, 168 left, 196-97 top gutter, 197 center right

Library of Congress: 11 bottom, 23 bottom, 30-31, 36 top left and right, 37, 71 top, 189, 200 top right

Mrs. F. C. Longworth: 85

Shirley Chudnow Malitz: 125 left, 145 bottom, 197 bottom

McCullough Models: 68 bottom, 87, 163 left

Jimmie McCullough: 139 bottom left and right

Laura McEvoy: 120 bottom

Barney McGinley: 191 top

Robert Malmstrom: 93 left, 104 top

Jeffrey Marinoff: 9 top, 14 bottom

William Martino, Jr.: 124 inset

Dr. James H. Mason: 6, 58 top

Merv Griffin's Resorts Casino Hotel: 207

Peter Miller: 138 top right, 139 top

Miss America Pageant, Inc.: 158 right, 162 left, 163 right, 171

Dawn Moiras: 152 top

Marie Morgan: 88 inset

Goerge Moss Jr.: 58 bottom

Newark Public Library: 109 bottom, 175 bottom

New Jersey Historical Society: 10-11

Reese Palley: 185

Parker Brothers, Division of Hasbro: 195, 198 bottom, 199

Ruth C. Patterson: 164

Adrian Phillips: 111, 162 right

Playboy Enterprises: 41 top, 206 bottom

Princeton Antiques: 42

Republic Pictures: 128 bottom

Resorts International Hotel formerly the Chalfonte-Haddon Hall: 44 bottom, 200 bottom left

Floyd and Marion Rinhart: 4 inset

Bert Rothman: 43 full page

George W. Rowland: 121 right

Ada Taylor Sackett: 74 left

Sands Hotel and Casino: 207

Save Lucy Committee, Inc.: 71, 72 bottom left

Lillian Schwartz: 41 bottom right, 49

Allyn Seel: 19

Showboat Casino and Hotel: 207

Joe Smith: 122 bottom

Ely Stevens: 25

Mr. and Mrs. G. W. Swatsworth: 101 top

Theatre Collection of the New York Library: 122 top

The Press of Southern New Jersey: 50-51, 53, 63 inset, 67 inset, 175 right, 193 left

The Saturday Evening Post © 1939 Curtiss Publishing: 193 inset

TropWorld Casino and Entertainment Resort: 206

Trump's Castle Casino Resort: 207

Trump Plaza Hotel and Casino: 206

Trump Taj Mahal Casino Resort: 207

Sidney Trusty: 137

Twentieth Century-Fox: 128 top

U.P.I./Bettman: 68 top, 108 top and bottom, 109 bottom, 169 left

Rudy Vallée: 131, 142 top

Milt Wescoat: 190

White House Sub: 151 left

Kirby White: 40 top left and right

Wide World Photos: 168 right, 123 top, 192 left and right

Ziegfeld Club: 120 top right

MOMENTS TO REMEMBER (pages 97-100):

Snapshots courtesy of: Mrs. Floyd M. Bishop, Ruth Cupples, Lynda Dees, Elsie Kendis, Claire Shorngold, Sidney Trusty, Bugsy Vlados

ALBUM OF FAMILIES (pages 114-117):

Snapshots courtesy of: Joseph Broski, Harel Cohen, Susan Subtle Dintenfass, Marc Gold, Valerie Gold, Edith and Ralph Green, Eve Greenfield, Marilyn Gardner Hamburger, Dolores Goldstein Jaffe, Audrey Hart, Elsie Kendis, Rod Kennedy, Vicki Gold Levi, Rose Levine, Chloe Price, Lillian Price, Mrs. Delbert Quammen, Terry Read, H. M. Saffer II

COVER:

Steve Lawrence, opening day of gambling: Courtesy of Merv Griffin's Resorts Casino Hotel

Mary Ann Mobley, Miss America, 1959: Courtesy of Miss America Pageant, Inc.

Arctic Avenue Easter Parade: Courtesy of Jeanette Hall

Mr. Peanut: Photo by Mark Haven

Sonora Carver on Red Lips: Photo by Kelso Taylor, courtesy of Arnette and Jake French

Lucy the Elephant: Courtesy of the Historical Society of Pennsylvania

BACK COVER

Lobster Ladies: Photo by Charles K. Doble, Sr.

INDEX